T0248080

salvage

ALSO BY DIONNE BRAND

Dionne Brand

Salvage

Readings from the Wreck

Farrar, Straus and Giroux
New York

Farrar, Straus and Giroux
120 Broadway, New York 10271

Printed in the United States of America
Originally published in 2024 by Alfred A. Knopf Canada
Published in the United States by Farrar, Straus and Giroux
First American edition, 2024

A version of the chapter "An autobiography of the autobiography
of reading" was delivered and published as a Kreisel Lecture
2019, 2020 respectively.

Library of Congress Cataloging-in-Publication Data
Names: Brand, Dionne, 1953– author.
Title: Salvage : readings from the wreck / Dionne Brand.
Description: First American edition. | New York : Farrar, Straus and
  Giroux, 2024. | Includes bibliographical references.
Identifiers: LCCN 2024019164 | ISBN 9780374614843 (hardcover)
Subjects: LCSH: Brand, Dionne, 1953– —Books and reading. | Black
  people in literature. | Imperialism in literature. | Racism in literature. |
  LCGFT: Autobiographies. | Literary criticism.
Classification: LCC PS8553.R275 Z46 2024 | DDC 811/.54 [B]—
  dc23/eng/20240429
LC record available at https://lccn.loc.gov/2024019164

Designed by Dylan Browne
Typeset by Sean Tai

www.fsgbooks.com
Follow us on social media at @fsgbooks

1   3   5   7   9   10   8   6   4   2

Contents

To recover belongings from a wreck

There is a painting by the Eritrean American artist Ficre Ghebreyesus named *Solitary Boat in Red and Blue*.[1] It is a painting I find utterly compelling, utterly seductive—perhaps because I love the colour blue, and who doesn't? But I find the blue and this painting so luminous, so doubled. Ghebreyesus's boat drifts on an opalescent bluish green sea along a smoke-bush green, emerald sky. The boat has an ethereal appearance, its reflection drifting below in the water; its destination is everywhere. It gestures to another reality of boats—boats that we know about, distressed in the Mediterranean or the Atlantic. I want to be in Ghebreyesus's boat and perhaps I am; it has such light in it, and is such an invitation to uncertainty and bounty. I once wrote, "even a wrecked and wretched boat still has all the possibilities of moving."[2] But *Solitary Boat in Red and Blue* is not a wrecked boat. It is the spirit of boats that I spoke of in those lines. It is a boat moving with all haste, languor and possibility. It is two boats, three boats, in combination with one's own illusive boat: solid, reflective and imagined. The moths or fireflies that accompany the boat with their own grey blue translucence almost seem to be floating on water themselves. And where is the boat going, I ask? And the answer, it seems, is to somewhere green. Its lightness and drift indicate its whereabouts and destination. I can't get enough of the painting. One's eyes are always rewarded and that is because of its movement. If you glance away, you find it at another place, at a new place. "Solitary" is paradox here.

There is another painting of a boat that I love, Remedios Varo's *Exploration of the Sources of the Orinoco River*.[3] A woman, Varo's avatar, sits in a red, fish-like bucketed waistcoat of a boat. She arrives in this boat at the source of the Orinoco only to find, whimsically or ironically, a coffee table with a glass spilling wine that appears to be the beginning of the river. In the painting, metaphor becomes a critique of such explorations: they resulted only in super-consumption and exploitation.

Unlike Varo's painting, Ghebreyesus's *Solitary Boat in Red and Blue* has no destination so specific and no purpose so directive and acquisitive. Nor one so ironic. There is no one on board, yet it seems everyone we wish to be, or know, is on board; so perhaps someone *is* on board. Whatever the case, this boat's intentions are not missionary, with all the attendant violent and coercive relations that go along with "discovery" and "exploration" for future uses; it does not seek information or commodifiable knowledge. It is not equipped with a compass. And the end of its journey is still open to wonder.

One hears of shipwrecks, many shipwrecks. Not massive container ships like the *Ever Given*[4] which ran aground in the Suez Canal,[5] nor the ten-deck, thousand-foot-long cruise ships that move tourists around the world. Not those centuries-old wrecks, popular in literature, that emanated from what was called the *voyage* and the *adventure*. Not the shipwrecks where gold and treasure are lost; not those wrecks from that violent age, whose treasures are still sought today by modern adventurers with "scientific methods." In the shipwrecks I hear of, there is another loss at sea. Human. These wrecks are of small vessels that move people and their precarity across the Mediterranean, the Strait of Gibraltar, the Atlantic and the Gulf of Mexico. These are the boats and the pirogues and the dinghies, full of people who are trying to land in safety, but who might be interdicted and pushed back in the other direction. Or drowned. Or: arrived, only to be held again on some ship—the *Bibby Stockholm*[6]—much like the Convict Hulks[7] of eighteenth- and nineteenth-century London.

There are many shipwrecks now. They are attended by border and security regimes; they end in loss of lives. The salvage there, in wrecked pirogues, is bodies, small possessions, wallets, cell phones, T-shirts, raincoats, jackets, keys to houses and rooms, sodden papers, only valuable to the ones who lost their lives. And to those who wait for word of their safe landing. A Tunisian fisherman, Oussama Dabbebi, says, "Instead of getting fish, I sometimes get dead bodies. The first time I was afraid, then step by step I got used to it. After a while getting a dead body out of my net is like getting a fish. Once I found a baby's body. How is a baby responsible for anything?"[8] These lives were/are animated by need and want, and not by adventure. These lives were/are destroyed by need and want and the adventures of totalizing forces, of multinational arrangements, oil concessions, cocoa concessions, lumber concessions, mineral concessions, toxic waste concessions and electronic waste concessions.

Those earlier shipwrecks contained the precarious too—the enslaved. But most of the stories that arrive from those times, and propel modern adventurers, are ones of lost wealth/treasure, such as that of the Spanish fleet sunk by a hurricane in the eighteenth century: fifty million dollars' worth of gold coins and gold chain recovered, and an estimated four hundred million more still hiding in the sea, they say. And along with the gold bullion were the enslaved, who were also treasure to be transformed into more gold.

J.M.W. Turner's oceans, explosions of movement and colour, perhaps hint at this catastrophe below. *Slavers Throwing Overboard the Dead and Dying, Typhoon Coming On* (1840)[9] is the most searing of these paintings, although any Turner ocean is tumultuous. Yet *Slavers* best evokes the indifference fuelling the cataclysm that overtook millions of abducted, enslaved and transported Africans—an indifference that drove Turner's watercolours to their experiments, no doubt. And a haunting that lead John Ruskin to use the word "blood" twice, but never once "human" or "slavery," in his high praise for Turner's *Slavers*. Even though, that "blood" is "girded with condemnation in that fearful hue which signs the sky with horror," as Ruskin writes.[10]

As I write, it is four years since the beginning of the Covid-19 pandemic, and throughout this time the boats kept/keep leaving and arriving even as the pandemic itself, its enormity, still may not have struck all of us, except in moments and on days when we cannot believe how much time has passed since something quite unknown—though, we suspect, inevitable and truly uncontrollable—entered our lives. And not only our lives—as so often when we say "our lives" we mean only our social worlds—but our very biological viability. Increasingly we suspect what has entered is something irreparable, something irreversible, undoable. Like wreckage. And those of us who see the wreckage feel like unwanted messengers about the crisis already, always in progress. We recognize the deterioration of the geological life of the planet itself to be irreparable; the coincidence of great human migration and deep geological crisis is not lost on some of us. The migrations from South to North have everything to do with exploitation of the South by the North. Nihilistic resource extraction creates physically, socially and politically uninhabitable conditions. But those are broad terms: "North" and "South." Interrelated interests abound in capital. Those of us who live in the South know this complexity well, and those of us who live in the North know it, too—though the blindfold of metropolitan superiority mostly obscures or ignores that knowledge. Whoever "we" are, the passage of this time, these past few years, has been like walking deeper and deeper into a space whose full contours we are still making out. We have run into something. What? And who is "we"?

Capital has slingshot back, and seems to have accelerated in its motion, making up and superseding what it calls its losses over the last years. The pandemic has left the headlines, and we are back to "normal." Or, "normal" quadrupled, which is to say more extraction, more war—the most rapid means of growth of capital; and more designation/eradication of the human beings extraneous and dispensable to the project of "normal." "Normal," it must be concluded, is nihilism-capital, churning up disasters geological and human, since that is all "we" are getting back to. This "we" insists on an aggregate of some kind; but something is always happening to its signification. This "we" that we have all been drafted into has collected around a set of social behaviours that have been made into principles. It is a "we" that takes the historical trajectory of the present dominant economic configuration, with its conflicts, tensions and contradictions, for granted. This dominant ideology sweeps the boats aside like so much anticipated death, like personal or cultural failures. It calls these migrations the fault of failed states, not the brutal expulsions necessary to the new global political economy. These are what Saskia Sassen names, in her book *Expulsions: Brutality and Complexity in the Global Economy*,[11] the "elementary brutalities" that attend the so-called complex economies.

This pronoun "we" that we invoke is, at base, a "we" of constant, detailed and expanding consumption, refracting in geopolitical and historical ways. All of us are recruited into this "we," whether we *have* the means, or whether we *are* the means by which others extract and consume.

"We" and "us" are always in flux. The meanings disaggregate with self-consciousness. "We" is an aggregate already disaggregated. And even in that partiality there is disaggregation.

We were made still by the pandemic. We were made still, and we could observe the great movement, the articulation of who was "we" and who was "we."

In the global North we were forced to come to terms with the rest of world. Not as labour pool, waste dumping site, theatre of war, arena of resource extraction; not as Globalization— meaning the complete annexing of the world's resources and labour supply in the project of neo-liberal capitalism. Rather, a broad "we" in the global North briefly felt the way it is to live in the global South—under siege, under lack, under restraint. The world folded like cloth or like paper into the uncomfortable recognition of the "we"—of its geological whole. We suddenly felt the earth as if our feet were on the same shaky surface. The earth compressed its air and time together—and briefly made all distinctions superfluous. We went from world to earth to planet, and we realized the planet is indifferent to us. It goes on in any incarnation—it will sweep us away, it has no stake in us, it has no compassion. The pandemic allowed us to see and think; or forced us to see and think; or forced others among us to refuse to see and refuse to think—and it occurred to some of us that this is what it must have felt like for decades somewhere else. This was not some accustomed tragedy happening elsewhere, but everywhere; and for a short while "we" were not someone else, but everyone. Or: we were all someone else; and those of us who were someone else wherever we were, anyway—well, we were everyone *and* someone else as we always had been. The world altered. The global North could not distribute its usual knowing looks of pity and blame, divorced from its complicity in the conditions that emanate from our/its way in the world. We stopped. For a short time, that is, or for as long as most memory lasts in the global North—until the stock markets corrected themselves; until commentators reclaimed the racist narratives of difference. For a short time, we, or many of us, were stilled—until the supply lines figured out their new and old trajectories.

But this world-stillness hovers anyway; it is pressing over everyone and someone, over the indifferent planet; this world-stillness overrides and catapults, despite our ongoing right-siding toward a killing, stratifying, death-dealing normal. It is a stillness we encounter between every moment of living now; a stillness that cannot be described by the markets and the supply lines and the dominant interpretation of the normal; a stillness from whose attentions we cannot be reclaimed fully or returned to that dominant interpretation. In this stillness, we surmise that we must attend to some urgency in the process of defining itself.

Early in this season of stillness, this season of observation, when commentators and reporters tried to collect us into the generalizable "we," to breathe confidence into the faltering project of "we" in order to keep our spirits up, they asked, "How should we get through this time?"; and "What should we read to get us through?" They asked, "Has any writer provided us with a key, to understand, to transform; to escape this time; to cope?"; "Does the literary canon contain any balm, any advice?" The implied question was, Did a certain set of Euro or Anglo-American texts provide a roadmap to the way through and the way out? This, of course, pointed directly to the aggregate "we," the one that coalesces into whiteness, or the genre of the human whose precondition is whiteness. And right on time, someone wrote in the *Guardian*: "What We Can Learn from Elizabeth Barrett Browning's Years in Lockdown." The essay went on to read: "After being diagnosed with a severe respiratory illness, the poet was forced to live in isolation. Her response offers great insights into how to cope. Lockdown taught her actively to embrace the freedom to travel when it came." (And isn't this just where "we" are now, and why the planet will continue to heave? And just who can travel in this time?) The commentator continued, "Yet the same material was also offering me a fascinating insight into how to cope with what was going on in my own world.... Her grasp of self-invention through a kind of 'second life' reminded me of all the friendships we were suddenly reconfiguring on Zoom. I also realized how closely her practice prefigured today's digital communicators: not just the teenagers and geeks, bloggers and TikTok stars, but citizen journalists, activists and those policed by authoritarian regimes too."[12] (I wryly note here "second life," and its resonance with that eponymous online game in which one creates an avatar and interacts with others.) The writer is trying to make some connection, to draw a line from the past to the present, but that's just it: this connection is through whiteness—the white "we," metonym for every "we," innocently, casually summoned.

In fact, we *are* summoned through the bourgeois life of nineteenth-century England: we are lathered in slaveholding and the fortunes made in enslavement. This summons arrived in the global North, in the middle of the pandemic, whole and aspirational, and as exemplar—as juridical in its demand. Naturally, if the world was falling apart during the pandemic, then its constitutive elements were also under siege; and if one of those elements was whiteness, then its tropes, its narrative history, needed shoring up. Its narrative proprietorship needed affirming. Or more innocently, the narrative apparatus that undergirded and attended its dominance rallied in its defence.

Harriet Jacobs never came to mind for the *Guardian* commentator, I observed. Nor did the enslaved woman who is the narrator of Browning's 1848 poem "The Runaway Slave at Pilgrim's Point." Elizabeth Barrett Browning, whose family fortune was made through slavery in Jamaica, lived at the same time as Harriet Jacobs, who spent seven years hiding in a crawlspace three feet high by nine feet wide by seven feet long, escaping Dr. Norcom, the white man who claimed ownership over her. She would publish, in 1861, *Incidents in the Life of a Slave Girl: Written By Herself*.[13] In this slave narrative she would recount her years in slavery, her seven years in confinement, and then her years in the north working to get her children free. Perhaps *this* is the text we should read for knowledge for surviving. Perhaps we should look for lessons at what Jacobs described as her "loophole of retreat"[14] (taken up so brilliantly by the sculptor Simone Leigh); perhaps we should look to Jacobs for an understanding of how to survive the crushing enclosure, and the existential void, for how to imagine and make real something like freedom.

I immediately thought, too, of all the writers I had read through the long time of our enduring, through outlasting the racism that brackets our lives, and hovers over all endeavours, presaging all appearances and events. And I found myself perplexed by these references to a literary canon that had surely tried to excise, by enclosure and confinement, Black experience in the Atlantic world by continually reproducing only white bourgeoise experience as "meaning." But, more innocently, my immediate reaction was of astonishment—as one is always astonished in this long durée of slavery and colonialism. "Goodness," I thought. "Read any writer in the Black Tradition and you will see how to get through. Or writers from the geopolitical South who also must find a way through and around the glutinous 'we.'"

Read *Beloved*, by Toni Morrison, where Sethe and Paul D survive slavery and navigate, attentively, their lives in the still fulminating anti-Black rage of Reconstruction and its brutal end.

Read, in Tsitsi Dangarembga's *Nervous Conditions*, of Tambu, Nyasha, Babamukuru, Lucia and others whose lives are under pressure as one cosmology forcibly eclipses another. Read Sam Selvon's *The Lonely Londoners*, where thousands emigrated by boat to London from the Caribbean, understanding their changing position and navigating this with humour and seriousness and everything that must be brought to bear in order to survive empire in the heart of empire. Read Edwidge Danticat's *The Farming of Bones*, where Haitian people in the Dominican Republic, over the course of seven days in 1937, experienced a genocide under Trujillo. In that novel, Amabelle Désir survives with compassion, having lost her lover and those around her. Read John Keene's sweeping diasporic *Counternarratives*,[15] which moves from the seventeenth century into the present, from Juan Rodrigues in the story "Mannahatta" to the speakers in the unnamed post-colonial interrogation room in the story "The Lions." Read these works to understand how sustained, intense pressure shuts a life down, curtails its movement, makes all plans indefinite, shapes all days, yet does not frame its purpose. Read there about waiting. Read there about patience and cunning and imagination and laughter.

So many novels in Black Traditions are novels of endurance and survival through times of material and existential dread and confinement. So many recount surviving and enduring with compassion, with resolve, with knowledge, with humour and a determination to live otherwise. These texts (novels, stories) come out of, metabolise, and work in, the world of nihilistic extraction. Their imaginative field is the great catastrophe that undergirds what we call the Americas. Over a reading life I have sought out and read these works as a salve, as a balm, as a map, as a trace, as an analysis, as a hypothesis, about the coming of freedom from within what is circumscribing and possibly fatal. A world is always ending in these books. A world is about to begin in these books, or about to be forestalled; about to, but not guaranteed to, "be" in these books. And this is the sensorium they chart. The novels' outcomes are living—when dying, of course; but living as if living.

The wreck is the library itself, and the salvage is the life which exceeds the wreck. Exceeds this library. *Solitary Boat in Red and Blue* exceeds the fragile boats, and renders the full desires they carry and hold.

So, I ask myself, what is a life alert in this sensorium and animated by books, as mine has been? What is a life making its way through this *monopoly of interpretation* (as Fredric Jameson calls it) that colonial narratives represent? Well, it might be a life animated but also destroyed by books—that is, animated but also destroyed by stories that override life, that overlay experience, that deny experience or quantify experience or adjust experience. What is that life? A life animated by books is something that everyone may understand, but a life destroyed by books is the more complex, contradictory, mysterious proposition. The wreck is, of course, possibly a life.

I observe, and live through, the monopoly of interpretation that relegates the art of those who live through catastrophe to spectacle or pathology, and into a symbol of the always not "we." Not art. Not an assemblage of the materials of perception that appraise and know life and what is lived. Not a set of insights and gestures of transformation. So the risk of going forward here is the risk of being read by some in this way. When I use the autobiographical, it is as artifice. It is not an invitation to witness transparency. Where it appears, it will have been pored over, turned over, analyzed, refashioned as art, and made theoretical through those processes. The only place the autobiographical appears in my art with a small vestige of itself may be in the fictions that I write. And even then, alloyed.

This book is another kind of forensics. A forensics of how a reader is made. And, unmade. A forensics of the literary substance of which I am made—since it is possible that I am now mostly literary substance—and that I must recover from; and if not recover from, then piece together.

An autobiography of the autobiography of reading

I. an appearance

There is a photograph of me taken when I was a child. I do not recognize myself, though I seem to remember the day and the event. The little girl, reputed to be me, in the photograph is about three or four years old. It is the only photograph of this period. They say that I am one of the four children in this photograph; the three others are my sisters and my closest cousin. I recognize *them*. We are four girls. I am alleged to be second from the left, third from the right. We all have white ribbons in our hair. We are taking a photograph to send to England to my mother and her younger sister, who are there becoming nurses. Several years before, they had left by boat, by ship, perhaps a Cunard ship,[16] whose name my aunt does not now recall, though she does recall passing Tenerife, standing on deck—thinking that one day she would like to go back there. She says this even today with the same longing as she did then. Over the phone in the present, Tenerife is vivid in her recollection as a site of beauty, another world. They arrived at the port of Southampton, my aunt and my mother, sometime in 1956. From Southampton they took a boat-train to London, where they were gathered by the hospital they'd been assigned to. This boat-train I meet later in the wonderful first sentence of Samuel Selvon's novel *The Lonely Londoners*: "One grim winter evening, when it had a kind of unrealness about London, with a fog sleeping restlessly over the city and the lights showing in the blur as if is not London at all but some strange place on another planet, Moses Aloetta hop on a number 46 bus at the corner of Chepstow Road and Westbourne Grove to go to Waterloo to meet a fellar who was coming from Trinidad on the boat-train."[17]

I imagine that my mother and my aunt encountered this same London as described by Selvon. When we take the photograph, we are taking it to send to my mother and my aunt, but also to send to England. England is in the air at home. It is referred to with reverence as "away" or "abroad." England is as much the recipient as my mother and my aunt; and for England, standing behind my mother and my aunt, we must make a good appearance. They arrived in London under the impression that they, too, had to make a good appearance, so that they and we would be accepted and acceptable. The girl, said to be me, is to my mind, the most active person in the photograph, helping the photographer to make the photograph right. I remember my younger sister and cousin crying and the photographer, Mr. Wong, assigning me to distract them with a toy rattle. I take my job seriously. Although now, it seems to me, mechanically. We must look out into the camera, Mr. Wong says. "Little girls, smile! Don't cry." I recall trying to follow his instruction; my little sister is crying, and my cousin is trembling in sympathy. My older sister is aloof with her own self-arrangement. I remember all these actions, but I do not recognize the girl who is me in the photograph. Whomever I appear to be is simply that: an appearance—as when you come upon a figure across the street reflected in a glass-walled building. Or even more remote than that; I cannot make out any gestural similarity between us. Except for my older sister, we children do not remember my mother and my aunt. We three youngest only know of them from stories, from the frequent invocation of their names in the house where we live. My mother and my aunt are in the imagination and so, too, is England, where they now live and where they are said to be getting along. We are all tied to England, and England to the imagination. All letters after this—all communication of information, endearment and entreaty—will go to and arrive from Wandle Valley Hospital, Mitcham Junction, Surrey, England. Sixty years later my older sister will still remember this address by heart. And all the letters, back and forth, will begin with this courtesy: *Dear _____, Hope you are well and enjoying the best of health*. England will be the recipient, the audience. England is the better place. Our lives will revolve around and be decided in the letters sent and received.

Everyone says the little girl looks like me. I doubt it. I do not recognize myself. Already I am changed in the photograph, since I leave off being myself to follow the directive of the photographer; already I have changed, thinking of composing myself for the audience. I now recognize myself as authored, altered. As selected, sorted, from a series of selves, for appearance and presentation. All photographs are like this, of course. One is conscious or anxious or confident or deliberate in striking an appearance that must keep, must transmit one's meaning—or the photographer's meaning. That is the studium, as Barthes describes in *Camera Lucida*—and that photograph is supposed to reach its viewers and reassure them. And it probably does. Though we four children are without conscious meaning, which is why we are crying or aloof or attentive to the photographer—and that is the punctum. The photograph, or the job the photographer must do, is disrupted by the indecorousness of some of the subjects, the disparate attitudes of the little girls who, despite being told of the importance and expense of the occasion of the photograph, respond in wholly individual ways. They do not even mean to disrupt; they have been warned not to be ill behaved, as I recall. But they've panicked in the face of these disciplines. They are panicked by the stranger who is the photographer, the new-linoleum smell of the room where the photograph is being taken, the tripod, the camera, the warning to behave and the shy desire to have themselves be seen by the mother and the aunt in England. Ultimately, the photograph can't do all the work it is required to do: the photograph does produce the likenesses of the children, but they themselves are in the middle of being something—they are still pliable, permeable; you can see all that in the photograph—and that disrupts the work the photo is being sent out to do. They are/we are not properly composed. The photo also perhaps confirms the disciplining work still to be done. Despite Mr. Wong's arrangement of us by height, despite his angles and the curtain behind and the linoleum floor composition, the photo cannot hold the girls in. And perhaps we will remain in this liminal space between photograph and meaning—permeable. But perhaps not.

The permeability evident in the photograph will yield to instruction from here on—instruction that also arrives from

English school books, English academic testing, English literature that a colonial apparatus provides. I will go on to Mrs. Greenidge's Dame School, I will go on to the San Fernando Girls' English Catholic School, I will go on to the Naparima Girls' High School, sending letters and receiving instructions from England; from Surrey, then from Croydon; then from *Pip and the Convict, Dick Whittington and His Cat,* "Bobby Shafto's Gone to Sea," "To a Butterfly," "Oh Mary, go and call the cattle home/ . . . Across the sands o'Dee"—becoming, becoming the representation of the self, signified by the opportunity of the photographic event.

A photograph. A portrait, desired, settled and puncturing the frame of the photograph. All the relations that come together to make the portrait—the children; the mother and the aunt waiting for the photograph; the adult outside of the frame who brought the children here to take the photograph; the photographer, who has taken many such photographs to send to mothers and aunts and fathers and sisters; England, observing these children over the shoulders of mothers and aunts. This porous portrait is full of multiple autobiographies: Mr. Wong, the photographer, probably traces his family to Chinese indentured labour—from 1846, or perhaps even as far back as 1806 (Indian indentured labour, beginning in 1845, also makes up the historical in the town where the photography studio operates); the children, whose history goes back to the period of Arawak/Carib extermination and the enslavement and transportation of their families from West Africa to the New World. All of these meet in a photography studio to follow a custom marked at every step with colonial imperative. All of these violent trajectories are synthesized in the photograph. The act of taking the photograph is deeply calculated to "arrive," to align with the imperative. It is an attempt to "appear," to synchronize with coloniality's time of modernity, of proper subjectivity.

I call this part of *Salvage* "An Autobiography of the Autobiography of Reading," leading with the indefinite "an autobiography" and leaving open the possibility of multiple autobiographies, of which this is but one iteration; it is particular but not individual. The indefinite article makes it one account, yet not one that is stable. The fissile materials of its construction through coloniality leave open molecular changes that may generate numerous autobiographies. Alongside this indefinite "*an* autobiography" another might be made, produced simultaneously. Which is to say, this should not be mistaken for the account of my life but an analysis of reading. *An* autobiography gestures to the world of a reading self. It signals the complicated ways of reading and interpretation that are necessary under conditions of coloniality. It suggests that coloniality constructs outsides and insides—worlds to be chosen, disturbed, interpreted and navigated—so as to live something like a real self. Which is to say, I could have been someone else. I could have drowned in the volume; I could have been buried under the weight. I could have suffocated, gasping in the toxicity of the atmospheres of coloniality. The definite article of the second clause, "the autobiography," identifies the subject who is supposed to be made through colonial pedagogies in the form of texts—fiction, non-fiction, poetry, photographs, governmental and bureaucratic structures. This subject, situated where violent pasts and futures of coloniality meet, is hailed in these texts so as to be governed with violence and erasure, and to suppress the understanding of that governance as violence and erasure.

II. unseen, unread

The great polymath—historian, novelist, critic and political scientist—C.L.R. James begins his elegant book on cricket and literature and politics, *Beyond a Boundary*, with a chapter called "The Window." In it he describes the window of his childhood house at the turn into the twentieth century—through this window he could see the cricket pitch of the town of Tunapuna. There, at six years old, he spent many Saturday hours standing on a chair and watching men practise the art of cricket. He also describes a childhood of reading incessantly—in particular, William Thackeray's *Vanity Fair*. James writes: "Thackeray, not Marx, bears the heaviest responsibility for me."[18]

Thackeray, not Marx, bears the heaviest responsibility for me. Scholars have gone over this line of James's with varying interpretations. Among these interpretations is that James was throwing shade on Marx, but if one reads the sentences before that one, one might approximate a truer answer. "I laughed without satiety at Thackeray's constant jokes and sneers and gibes at the aristocracy and at people in high places."[19] Here, James credits Thackeray with exposing the hypocrisy of the nineteenth-century British aristocracy. And he responds with the alternate knowledge of a man historically on the other side of that aristocracy. James continues: "But the things I did not notice and took for granted were more enduring: the British reticence, the British self-discipline, the stiff lips, upper and lower. When Major Dobbin returns from India, and he and Amelia greet each other, Thackeray asks: Why did Dobbin not speak? . . . George Osborne writes a cold, stiff letter to his estranged father before going into battle, but he places a kiss on the envelope, which Thackeray notes that his father did not see."[20] Here, James points to the British mores promulgated at the time, mores that were to become tropes in the national consciousness, tropes that James was inculcated in, despite their glaring contradictions. Then there are his passages about colonial teaching practices in the colonized world: "Not only the English masters, but Englishmen in their relation to games in the colonies, held tightly to the code as example and as a mark of differentiation."[21] Codes of moral rectitude, reserve, virtue and fair play were presented to the colonies as particularly British and ultimately unachievable, but necessary for the colonized to emulate. And here is James on the ways in which those codes of coloniality lay contradictorily and harshly on the colonized: "I was an actor on a stage in which the parts were set in advance. I not only took it to an extreme, I seemed to have been made by nature for nothing else. There were others around me who did not go as far and as completely as I did."[22]

James's *Beyond a Boundary* analyzes the game of cricket in order to set out the terms of coloniality laid down by the British, and then detail the acquisition and demolition of those terms through the game in the West Indies of the forties, fifties and sixties.

In the West Indies the cricket ethic has shaped not only the cricketers but social life as a whole. It is an understatement. There is a whole generation of us, and perhaps two generations, who have been formed by it not only in social attitudes but in our most intimate personal lives, in fact there more than anywhere else. The social attitudes we could to some degree alter if we wished. For the inner self the die was cast. . . . Along with restraint, not so much externally as in internal inhibitions, we learnt loyalty. It is good to be loyal to what you believe in—that, however, may be tautology. Loyalty to what is wrong, outmoded, reactionary is mischievous. To that in general all will agree, even the reactionary.[23]

Lisa Lowe in *The Intimacies of Four Continents* interprets James's formulation—that Thackeray, not Marx, made him—as James's appreciation of the way the novel describes the history of global empire: "Literature and culture mediated these early nineteenth-century world conditions, not by literally reflecting them in a fixed, transparent fashion, but rather by thematizing the manners in which imperial culture simultaneously recognized yet suppressed the emerging contradictions of the era. . . . Literature mediates these asymmetries of dominant, residual, and emergent forces, inasmuch as it may portray that such conditions were more often grasped as isolated effects, glimpsed in particular objects in the social fabric, rather than seized totally or framed systematically." Lowe gets at the work/ing of literature in the imperializing project, not as mere collateral uninterested effect, but as active, interested parts of the project.[24]

Mediated by literature, I think perhaps Thackeray, not Marx, made me too. Made me and unmade me. But perhaps, more importantly, James made me: his majestic book on the Haitian revolution, *The Black Jacobins: Toussaint L'Ouverture and the*

San Domingo Revolution; his novel *Minty Alley*; his political theory, *Notes on Dialectics*. These I would encounter parallel to and simultaneous with British novels. This was in the era of anti-colonialism—the Bandung Conference, the emerging independence movements. And when I read those lines of James's in *Beyond a Boundary*, they took me back to my own childhood and my first reading of *Vanity Fair*—back to Amelia Sedley, Becky Sharp, William Dobbin, Rawdon Crawley, George Osborne.

Like James, I read *Vanity Fair* first at a young age, perhaps twelve, and then in my twenties in a nineteenth-century literature class at university. The memory of my childhood reading does not bring (at least, not on the surface) lessons in restraint and the code of masculinity, or inhibition, or the great sprawl of that last colonial domination, ingested as the acceptable and inevitable, representing the fabric of social hierarchies, the material world itself. For me, the memory summons the codes and lessons of femininity. Amelia Sedley and Becky Sharp were thrown into stark moral relief—Amelia: gentle, rosy-cheeked, smiling, pliant and good; Becky: cunning, ungrateful, bitter and destined for no good. The narrative summoned me to attend to the example of Amelia Sedley, innocent and unconscious of the world, and therefore safe; and Becky Sharp, too worldly, too clever, too grasping, too knowledgeable, and therefore doomed. I was with Amelia, wanting her to be happy, wanting her to have Osborne, wanting Dobbin to take care of her. Why couldn't Becky *behave*?

As Thackeray himself says later, "Miss Sedley (whom we have selected for the very reason that she was the best-natured of all, otherwise what on earth was to have prevented us from putting up Miss Swartz, or Miss Crump, or Miss Hopkins, as heroine in her place?)—it could not be expected that every one should be of the humble and gentle temper of Miss Amelia Sedley; should take every opportunity to vanquish Rebecca's hard-heartedness and ill-humour; and, by a thousand kind words and offices, overcome, for once at least, her hostility to her kind."[25]

The obvious parody of femininity notwithstanding, because, after all, the outcome/alternative is unavailable as success in the text, I was called to choose. One suspected and feared the possibility of being Becky Sharp for other reasons. Becky Sharp gestured toward blackness in this respect of wanting what one did not have and growing bitter without it; of making out the project of becoming while being outside the project of becoming.

Then there was another figure, who appears on page 7 of my edition of *Vanity Fair*: "Miss Swartz, the rich woolly-haired mulatto from St. Kitt's . . ."[26] But I barely remembered her and only found her later, as a stunning surprise, on rereading. Thackeray also had a drawing of Miss Swartz, a drawing I must have decidedly forgotten or clinically forgotten, since to me, it was such a horrific drawing of a Black woman seemingly uncomfortable in cosquelle Victorian garb. Reading narrative requires, demands, acts of identification, association, affiliation, sympathy, and empathy, acts of inhabiting. And while James associated with and inhabited the faithful, loyal and restrained Dobbin, the heroic George Osborne, I inhabited the good, kind, gentle, somewhat insipid Amelia. (You must remember that "insipid" is one of the categories of femininity.) The geopolitics of empire had already prepared me for this identification, as it had prepared James for his—the goods, the information, the structures of bureaucracy, the physical colonial layout of place attenuating location, the systems of education in schools, language, manners—the hierarchies were already set out and therefore so were the ambitions. Or at least I was invited to inhabit Amelia by the mere presentation of her as innocence and goodness, silence, inaction and vapidity; and the acquisition of these traits as "character" in the text. Good character.

But how did I miss Miss Swartz? Why did I not inhabit Miss Swartz? Yes, she was not the main protagonist, but why did I forget her? And why on reading and rereading was Miss Swartz always a surprise to me? A shock that took me away from, disturbed, the narrative, and that threatened to impede it? And how, how did I miss on the very first page of *Vanity Fair* another figure, how did I read right past him? He was, after all, the opening mechanism for transporting all of Thackeray's text. He rang the bell to open the gates of Miss Pinkerton's academy, ushering the protagonists onto life's stage. And, of course, *Vanity Fair* is a parody, a critique of aristocratic Britain during this phase of imperialism. But imperialism escapes critique and blackness is doubly parodied. Because blackness *is* parody. So how did *I* miss Sambo? On the first page! What slippage of interpretation accomplished that? Why did I notice him only with dismayed recognition after years of inculcation in, then decompression from, imperialist aesthetics? Did I miss him, or take him, and Miss Swartz, for granted? Did I swallow them as the indigestible but necessary meal of coloniality on the way, nevertheless, to occupying and identifying with the colonial? For the text to work on this reader the way that it is supposed to, I cannot see Miss Swartz; I cannot remember her or Sambo. She, he, they, had to remain a perpetual surprise. Like the surprise of seeing myself that is not myself. I must have recognized Miss Swartz with disappointment as the representation of me, the stand-in for blackness and all its significations, and even as a child I understood them both, Miss Swartz and Sambo, to be without future in the narrative, and subject to horrifying sanctions.

Here is Sambo on the first page of *Vanity Fair*:

> While the present century was in its teens, and on one sunshiny morning in June, there drove up to the great iron gate of Miss Pinkerton's academy for young ladies, on Chiswick Mall, a large family coach, with two fat horses in blazing harness, driven by a fat coachman in a three-cornered hat and wig, at the rate of four miles an hour. A black servant, who reposed on the box beside the fat coachman, uncurled his bandy legs as soon as the equipage drew up opposite Miss Pinkerton's shining brass plate, and as he pulled the bell. . . .
> "It is Mrs. Sedley's coach, sister," said Miss Jemima. "Sambo, the black servant, has just rung the bell; and the coachman has a new red waistcoat."[27]

Again, I ask: how did I, on first reading, miss them? Or did I? Miss Swartz is mentioned thirty-six times. While her wealth as the daughter of a planter (who, we are told, is Jewish) and an undesignated Black woman (read: *enslaved*) does see her eventually married to aristocracy, throughout *Vanity Fair* Thackeray makes great play of her without suggesting what particular quality of hers we must make play with. He leaves us to arrive, as if on our own, at race, at blackness, as the laughable quality. Both Sambo and Miss Swartz are figures of the comic. The comic appears to position them in inverse relation to their actual importance to the economic obligations embedded in the narrative. Another figure, Loll Jewab, an Indian man who is a servant, in a farcical dismissal of India's importance to the colonial project is variously described as mistaken for the devil or having yellow eyes and white teeth. The names themselves—Sambo, Miss Swartz, Loll Jewab—are caricatures.

Thackeray's narrative schema, his arrangement of the elements of action, requires and places these figures as fixed, settled. Our reading and writing practices too—reading and writing as practices located within the ways we live and imagine ourselves in the world—admit and require this schema. We are as curious about these characters as we are about a necessary bit of described, denotative furniture. Which is to say, not at all. They enrich the text in crucial ways, but they do not live. Thackeray, after all, is writing this text in 1847; he is aware of his time, referring to the avarice of, without condemning or addressing, slavery, the slave trade, the exploitation of India and China. The mores of the British aristocracy are his main concerns, not colonial exploitation. And the novel is a scathing indictment of those mores. But nowhere does it indict what that wealth is built on. That wealth is a given—not the subject in question. I note here that Thackeray was born in India, his father a secretary of the East India Company.

Edward Said writes in *Culture and Imperialism*: "Nearly everywhere in nineteenth- and early-twentieth-century British and French culture we find allusions to the facts of empire, but perhaps nowhere with more regularity and frequency than in the British novel. Taken together, these allusions constitute what I have called a structure of attitude and reference."[28]

Thinking along with Said, *attitude* and *reference* as structure are embedded in the production of the novel during that time, in the form itself and in the structure of feeling intended to be produced by the novel. Everyone, meaning individuals and companies, had their hands in slavery and colonial exploitation, just as today individuals and corporations have their hands in extracting oil or minerals and producing electronics as they destroy the earth on which we live, and the oceans, waterways and air, while describing their actions in terms of jobs, livelihoods and wealth as a right of the rich.

So, I am talking about what comes to sit inside narrative writing (prose or poetry) as a result of the genesis, the action and long duration, of certain regimes in our material lives, certain relations of power, that make invisible or ordinary, or a given, those power relations. I am talking about how those very power relations are embedded in the structure and form of storytelling, reproducing the architecture of these regimes.

C.L.R. James would have seen this, as I did later: the aristocracy flush with money, their fortunes flowing; the deep effects of the Napoleonic Wars' control of territories in the New World;[29] the colonial conquest embedded in the book without any of the actors from those places speaking, but rather appearing as immutable. The action of *Vanity Fair* takes place during British slavery. (The writing of the novel takes place shortly after abolition.) Slavery is never mentioned in the text, but virtue, modesty, goodness and religion and God are. So, here is a society proceeding as if these things are divisible from enslavement. Conquest gives the narrative its velocity and moral reasoning—but it is the welfare of the conquerors that is at stake. Parody never undermines them.

For me, of course, the whole novel is immersed, steeped, in slavery. Of Lady Emily, Thackeray writes: "A mature spinster, and having given up all ideas of marriage, her love for the blacks occupied almost all her feelings. It is to her, I believe, we owe that beautiful poem—

> Lead us to some sunny isle,
> Yonder in the western deep;
> Where the skies for ever smile,
> And the blacks for ever weep, &c."

This so-called parody cannot overcome the sneer of "her love of the blacks occupied almost all her feelings." And one wonders what the parodic is in aid of here, except for cynical caricature. Thackeray may be talking about the superficiality of class and gender, but for me that is the glassy mirrored surface of violent narrative that one is watching and inhabiting, while underneath—actually, running throughout—is the pedagogy of colony. White class and white gender are being made here, and race and colony are central to that making; in fact, they are its normalized, stipulated and matter-of-fact bedrock.

The constant reinforcement of the unseen and unread throughout narrative, the hardening of the structural position of blackness within narrative, is the pedagogy of colony. Which brings me to Thackeray's *The History of Henry Esmond, Esq.*, an historical novel about the life of Henry Esmond, published in 1852. The time of the novel is the early eighteenth century. For my purposes, the story is not important. I want to look at the language—what it transmits, the state of being it describes, the mind, the philosophical orientation, of the speaker. I want to look at the language, which in this case is English, as vehicle—transporting ideas of the "normal" at the level of syntax and feeling, marking the relation of, and between, objects.

The History of Henry Esmond, Esq. begins:

> The estate of Castlewood, in Virginia, which was given to our ancestors by King Charles the First, as some return for the sacrifices made in His Majesty's cause by the Esmond family, lies in Westmoreland county, between the rivers Potomac and Rappahannock, and was once as great as an English Principality, though in the early times its revenues were but small. Indeed for near eighty years after our forefathers possessed them, our plantations were in the hands of factors, who enriched themselves one after another, though a few scores of hogsheads of tobacco were all the produce, that, for long after the Restoration, our family received from their Virginian estates.[30]

Notice the tenor of the paragraph, the relational claims it makes, the elevated stance of the speaker. Notice the emotive words it deploys—*return for the sacrifices*, *given to our ancestors*, *our forefathers possessed*. Note the invocation of the King, the words *great as an English Principality*, then the gesture to the wrongfully disadvantaged state of the family. All these words work to invoke regard and sympathy, and to summon association. To read this first paragraph is to read two worlds: the world being addressed, and the world buried in the address. So, let us look at other words and phrases in the text, their deployment and their effects: *Potomac and Rappahannock, our plantations, factors, hogsheads of tobacco.* This language is of objects, relating to the inanimate; or, in the case of *factors*, evoking two senses, figure/sums, accounts and advantage. But what do I read in the words *Potomac and Rappahannock* except Indigeneity and previous habitation—in fact, old habitation, if something like the name of a river is resistant to an English principality; and in *plantations* I read forced labour/enslavement of Black people—after all, we are in Virginia, which held claim to the seat of the Confederacy—and the labour exploited to produce hogsheads of tobacco. Suddenly my reading is populated by a great force of Black people unmentioned, moving about, living; and I become aware of their suffering. A set of exploitative relations now comes into view. But the vehicular language suspends the meanings and scale of this exploitation and human suffering, replacing them with a dreary tale of white disenfranchisement.

In his essay "Aesthetic Reflection and the Colonial Event: The Work of Art in the Age of Slavery," Simon Gikandi writes: "First, colonial events and subjects are never centered in the European discourse on the aesthetic, which dominates the 18th century, but they occupy important footnotes or addenda; if the aesthetic acquires its ideal character by its force of exclusion . . . it is, nevertheless, haunted by that which it excludes. . . . Since the end of the 18th century, debates about the aesthetic . . . [have been] concerned with the nature and judgement of beauty and explanation of artistic phenomena—and unconcerned with the turbulence associated with the colonial empire."[31]

Again, from *The History of Henry Esmond, Esq.*:

> Neither my father nor my mother ever wore powder in their hair; both their heads were as white as silver, as I can remember them. My dear mother possessed to the last an extraordinary brightness and freshness of complexion; nor would people believe that she did not wear rouge. At sixty years of age she still looked young, and was quite agile. It was not until after that dreadful siege of our house by the Indians, which left me a widow ere I was a mother, that my dear mother's health broke. She never recovered from her terror and anxiety of those days, which ended so fatally for me, then a bride scarce six months married, and died in my father's arms ere my own year of widowhood was over.[32]

I have to admit to reading this with cold-bloodedness—or at least, I cannot do what the reader is hailed to do, which is to juxtapose the refinement, good taste, beauty and rectitude of the mother, ergo England, against the dreadful siege and terror of the Indians. I cannot be the reader occupying "the" autobiography of reading. I cannot notice the brightness and freshness of complexion or see the lack of rouge as sacred. Instead, I admit to laughter and satisfaction at this siege and the early decease of the mother. Here, in Gikandi's formulation, the aesthetic must contend with the "turbulence associated with the colonial empire." To my great hilarity. That I say *I have to admit* and call myself cold-blooded, that I *admit to laughter* as if it isn't warranted, speaks to the presumption that the vehicular language has transported the pathos to the correct narrative subject, and that I am the reading subject who must respond to the material as if so transported—namely, through identification with the protagonist and some moral tenet, some tenet of proper aesthetic appreciation.

In the preface to the supposed memoirs of her father, Colonel Henry Esmond, Rachel Esmond Warrington writes:

> Though I never heard my father use a rough word, 'twas extraordinary with how much awe his people regarded him; and the servants on our plantation, both those assigned from England and the purchased negroes, obeyed him with an eagerness such as the most severe taskmasters round about us could never get from their people. He was never familiar, though perfectly simple and natural; he was the same with the meanest man as with the greatest, and as courteous to a black slave-girl as to the Governor's wife. No one ever thought of taking a liberty (except a tipsy gentleman from York, and I am bound to own that my papa never forgave him): he set the humblest people at once on their ease with him, and brought down the most arrogant by a grave satiric way, which made persons exceedingly afraid of him. His courtesy was not put on like a Sunday suit. . . . They say he liked to be the first in his company; but what company

was there in which he would not be first? . . . [He] had a
perfect grace and majesty of deportment, such as I have
never seen in this country. . . .[33]

To reiterate Gikandi, the aesthetic can never be sutured against
or cauterized from the "colonial event"; and even more than
that, I propose that the colonial event *is* the aesthetic—that its
pleasures, tastes, manners, consist of this juxtaposition. What
is pleasing, what is in beautiful form, *is* the violence. It is a possession; rather than being unpleasant or ugly, it is the desired
and valued commodity of an elevated mind, a good character.
It is the frisson, the jouissance in living life itself. The virtues
espoused cannot be separate from the moments of their production and description.

I don't have to point out the absurdity of the purchased
negroes obeying Esmond with eagerness just because he was
good and courteous, and of perfect grace, and possessing majesty
of deportment. But I do want to point out how we are being
hailed to enter a fantasy of relations, absent of power and the
violence that upholds it, regularized into the hierarchy. There
was an enormous production of this type of fiction/fantasy, all
of it transported by way of educational systems around the
English-speaking world, producing the way to read, and to read
the world, the way to live but also the way to imagine, the way
to write and the way to be. The way to feel.

III. the snarling . . . noise, and a deep human groan

I spent the first seventeen years of my life consuming this literature, passing through its sentences, absorbing its form, its structure, its aesthetic, and coming to know its rules of character, landscape, dialogue and so on.

In her essay "Novel and History, Plot and Plantation," Sylvia Wynter writes: "We [by which she means plantation or New World societies] are all, without exception, still 'enchanted,' imprisoned, deformed and schizophrenic in its [colonialism's] bewitched reality." And "the novel form and our societies are twin children of the same parents."[34]

A narratively constituted imaginary and existence are repeated, reinforced politically and socially, rewritten in every novel—either embedded there, or dug up to examine difference or those outside the narrative. Wynter describes an imaginary, a narrative schema in which blackness appears as immutable category. This narratively constituted imaginary is a code that considers itself ever-changing but is in fact ever-elaborating itself as primary—reconstituting the same materials in which it is primary, from which it deals out violence as empathy, violence as love, violence as the daily enactment of itself. Codes and algorithms, after all, are not neutral or value-free; they are embedded in, constitutive of, and produce sets of political and social relations—and, of course, literary ones.

Narrative is not just the simple construction of language, but the constitution and transportation of networks of feeling—how to feel and what to feel. It is intravenous to ideas of the self, and ideas of the self that contain negations of other people.

What is it, then, to adopt or be indoctrinated into those narrative structures, those ideas, to come to know those ideas as your own, when you are yourself the negated other people? When you are the intravenous being, the being administered into being as negation. For as Glissant writes in *Poetics of Relation*: "Imperialism (the thought as well as the reality of empire) does not conceive of anything universal but in every instance is a substitute for it."[35]

In an attempt at counteracting the toxicity of colonial narrative, I tried to practise a version of counternarrative in my 1988 short story "At the Lisbon Plate." After finding no name for the murdered man in Albert Camus's *L'Étranger / The Outsider*, I tried to imagine his day, his life before and when he encounters the colonial anxiety of Camus's Meursault, a colonial anxiety whose elaboration is the death of this man on the beach. I thought about how Camus un-names the victim and is unable or unwilling to fill out his life or hear his voice. And so, in a brief few paragraphs, I attempted in my early writing to fill in the register of existence, since the murdered man's life fell outside of the existential rhetoric of this period in French writing. The murdered man was outside of existentialism, or indeed constitutive of it, just as I was outside of and constitutive of colonial subjectivity. For Camus, even a grand proposition like existentialism could not contain the existence of the colonized. The discriminatory *Code de l'indigénat* in Algeria at the time of the novel is the unspoken "emptiness" of Meursault, the unspoken prerogative, unspoken in the text anyway, to appropriate anything from the "native," including life itself. "Ahmed. Ahmed. Ahmed," my story begins, naming the murdered man. "Ahmed came to the beach with Ousmane to get away.... He dropped the bicycle, raced Ousmane to the water.... Ahmed and Ousmane fell into the sea fully clothed, he washing away the sticky oil of the bicycle shop, Ousmane drowning his headache."[36] The story settles Ahmed into that day with his younger brother, Ousmane, telling of their getaway to the beach, carving a space away from the penury and the emergencies of the town and their lives.

I had read Camus wanting to learn the philosophy of existentialism. I had read his work trying to find some method of understanding, a way through, a path to that inclusive ideal of humanity. And I found instead that I had fallen out of the narrative. But then I understood it wasn't inclusion that I wanted. I wanted to be addressed.

And that brings me back to the "we"—also, to "an" and "the." "We" has a certain barbarity to it—a force. It is an administrative category; it is a gathering place of colonial/imperialist desires, and an apparatus for their workings. "We" binds the affective— the convivial sense of being in the world with other people—to the relations of ruling. Christina Sharpe says, "As one reads, one always encounters that curious 'we.' That 'we' constituted with no reference to one's own being—a 'we' made impossible by 'me.'"[37] To read is to encounter this "we" at every juncture, even when the word is not invoked, even when it is invoked in its most benign, well-meaning form. I ingested in those early years of reading the simultaneous summons and expulsion of "we." I felt the desire to enter, and the impossibility of entering.

Within this construct of "we," what is this reader to be but nothing, no being, not present, since the reader whose autobiography is being written is without present—without past and without future. A reader is being written with no character—a reader, inanimate, present as extension of "the being," "the character." That is to say, this reader experiences herself as a floating signifier in the narrative, perpetually escaping from and being captured in unwanted and unrecognizable signification.

During this time, of course, Jean Rhys's *Wide Sargasso Sea* served as a counternarrative to Charlotte Brontë's *Jane Eyre*. I imagine Rhys's autobiography of reading was similar to mine, at least in some partial way. And probably as an act of correcting the record or animating the inanimate in Brontë's text, Rhys created Bertha/Antoinette to trouble the narratively constituted imaginary. Brontë's *Jane Eyre* was published in the same year as, and just prior to, Thackeray's *Vanity Fair*. In fact, Brontë dedicates the second edition of *Jane Eyre* to Thackeray in admiration of his intellect and wit.

As a child I read *Jane Eyre*, and again later, as a university student. It is, above all, a novel about submission. Confinement and submission—zones of submission. All spaces in the novel are enclosures of female submission—the Reed house, the Lowood orphanage, Rochester's house—each a zone of submission and indoctrination to familial tyranny, institutional and religious doctrine, and white masculinity. The major ethical event is how Jane will resist or inhabit these zones of submission; the love plot is what follows. Necessary to the form of the nineteenth-century novel is the overcoming of (white) female social dissonance through romantic entanglement. The colonial event is hidden in *Jane Eyre*, albeit elaborating itself, and growling above, in the attic at Thornfield Hall. The violence, the plantation and slavery in Jamaica that make Thornfield possible—all are hidden. I have to think/extrapolate that every-day middle-class white experience in the nineteenth century must have been familiar with this growling for Brontë to have represented it. A one-paragraph summary mention of this centuries-long and ongoing event is performed three-quarters of the way through the novel. Perhaps Rhys, given her own relation to the colonial, in her reading of *Jane Eyre* would have been as alert to the hidden woman as she was alert to the fact that the colonial could not be sutured by the marriage plot.

Imprisoned in the attic is Bertha Mason, while underneath, in the drawing rooms and parlours, is the gaiety produced by the excesses of the plantation, the violence not regarded as violence and experienced as power, wealth and well-being. Thornfield Hall is animated by this sublimated violence. It is the expression of violence, a violence that everyone is aware of, that produces the excitement, the jouissance there. The house—filled with guests running to and fro, masquerading, playing charades—is a macabre space. We read:

> Everywhere, movement all day long. You could not now traverse the gallery, once so hushed, nor enter the front chambers, once so tenantless, without encountering a smart lady's-maid or a dandy valet.
>
> The kitchen, the butler's pantry, the servants' hall, the entrance hall, were equally alive; and the saloons were only left void and still when the blue sky and halcyon

sunshine of the genial spring weather called their occu-
pants out into the grounds. . . .

While Mr. Rochester and the other gentlemen directed these alterations, the ladies were running up and
down stairs ringing for their maids. Mrs. Fairfax was
summoned to give information respecting the resources
of the house in shawls, dresses, draperies of any kind; and
certain wardrobes of the third storey were ransacked . . .[38]

This busyness, this luxury, this aliveness is produced by the political economy of slavery. As a reader, hailed by its extravagance, I
did not at first notice the excess as excess. I only experienced the
abundance as wonderful; not until later did I experience it as
corrupt. The photograph I have described at the beginning of this
autobiography was itself a site of submission, from which, with
time and self-awareness and analysis, I would break free—break
free by attending to the lived contradictions that the photograph
contained. But meanwhile, the meta-data of the photograph
demanded affiliation with a protagonist such as Jane Eyre. The
meta-data says that the colonial world is the proper world, and
the photograph is a representation of the existence and dominance of that world. The reader who I was identified herself with
Jane—and though sidelined and tangential, I was not disapprov-
ing. The reader who I was wished that the woman, the chimera
in the attic, would not spoil things. The photograph, with its pat-
terned linoleum, its brown curtain, was its own chimeric attic.

It is only when Bertha Mason's brother arrives midway
through the novel that we get a hint, fleetingly, of the other life

upon which all this luxury is predicated. This is the first mention of colony, of "some hot country": "Presently the words Jamaica, Kingston, Spanish Town, indicated the West Indies as his residence; and it was with no little surprise I gathered, ere long, that he had there first seen and become acquainted with Mr. Rochester. He spoke of his friend's dislike of the burning heats, the hurricanes, and rainy seasons of that region."[39] It is deeply interesting how zones of exploitation are generally referenced and invoked in novels in general. Rainy seasons, burning heat, filth, distaste, poverty, disrepair, as if these words are metonyms. These words of course contain their own elisions. These zones are the zones that produce the enormous wealth of the protagonists and, while descriptively antagonistic, are zones of imperial desire and material claim. At the time in which *Jane Eyre* is set there are approximately 350,000 enslaved people in Jamaica and roughly 800 sugar plantations, to say nothing of coffee, cocoa and other products.

Soon after, when Mason is stabbed by his sister and Jane is enlisted to nurse him until Rochester gets the doctor, Jane hears "the snarling, canine noise, and a deep human groan. Then my own thoughts worried me. What crime was this that lived incarnate in this sequestered mansion, and could neither be expelled nor subdued by the owner?—what mystery, that broke out now in fire and now in blood, at the deadest hours of night? What creature was it, that, masked in an ordinary woman's face and shape, uttered the voice, now of a mocking demon, and anon of a carrion-seeking bird of prey?"[40]

Someone like me, reading, finds this a telling paragraph. It is amazingly put. Someone like me reads this snarling and deep human groan as the unconscious speaking, as the plantation come to England. This noise—the noise of the plantation world, the suppressed, the made-mad, the sequestered—was blackness. The deep human groan was the sound of millions of abducted and enslaved and worked-to-death Africans. And the crime that lived incarnate was slavery. This sequestered blackness would have travelled by boat (like my mother and my aunt, and thousands more who travelled to England in the fifties and sixties to labour) in other manifestations of the British psycho-social political economy.

After Rochester hurries the wounded Mason away before all is discovered, he speaks with Jane outside in the garden. We read: "He strayed down a walk edged with box, with apple trees, pear trees, and cherry trees on one side, and a border on the other full of all sorts of old-fashioned flowers, stocks, sweet-williams, primroses, pansies, mingled with southernwood, sweet-briar, and various fragrant herbs. They were fresh now as a succession of April showers and gleams, followed by a lovely spring morning, could make them: the sun was just entering the dappled east, and his light illumined the wreathed and dewy orchard trees and shone down the quiet walks under them. 'Jane, will you have a flower?'"[41]

The paragraph wobbles and teeters illogically away from what threatens to hold Brontë's hand. It is a most strange turn of narration—and yet one that is completely understandable, for where else could the narrative go, given its antiseptic colonial project? The trope of the English garden is employed here—however mannered and cultivated, this space gestures as the naturally pristine space; a space of gentility and finer feeling deployed against barbarity. But whose barbarity? This appeal to the English natural world—the beauty and quiet, the less-mad, the sane, the rightful order—is the justification for all that must be done to maintain the colonial order. England and the English psyche remain tranquil and uncontaminated.

When Jane eventually inherits—as she must, so that what is called the narrative arc is achieved—it is from her uncle, late of Madeira: Madeira, which was involved in the slave trade. Until then in the novel, Jane has stood relatively outside of the taint, outside a direct involvement with plantation/slave capital. But the granting of her full sovereignty can only be accomplished by her full immersion in plantation economics. At one time, Madeira had engaged in the production of sugar from sugar-cane using enslaved labour from Africa and the Canaries. At the time of the novel, having ended sugar production for want of resources to exploit, it is now a producer of wine. So, Jane's autonomy, her £25,000 per year so generously shared with her three cousins, is acquired through the same system by which Rochester acquires his money. The contentment that she feels, and that we are to feel for her, is riven with violence.

In *Wide Sargasso Sea*, Jean Rhys takes care of Rochester's brief account (those few words in Brontë's *Jane Eyre*) of his involvement with Bertha Mason, whose real name we come to know is Antoinette, her name changed by Rochester in an act of possession and right to name. In her act of counter-narration, Rhys un-names Rochester. While Rhys exposes the political economy of slaveholding, and how the marriage arrangement/plot buttresses these relations, she leaves unopened the fantasy of the enslaved's love for the master. The figure of Christophine in *Wide*

Sargasso Sea is inexplicable as protector and mother figure to Antoinette and her mother. A Black woman formerly enslaved by Antoinette's family presented as Antoinette's defender and protector against Rochester? A reader like me observes this. It is a deep contradiction yet a reader like me understands it as an enduring white trope. Christophine confronts Rochester about his true motives. "You think you fool me?" she asks him. "You want her money, but you don't want her. . . . You do that for money? But you wicked like Satan self!"[42] Christophine, in the years since emancipation and Antoinette's growing-up, has been imprisoned for being an Obeah woman and healer—a status crime of colonial times, since these women were usually at the forefront of fomenting rebellion. So while Rhys presents the figure of Christophine as a powerful one, Christophine's love and caring for Antoinette remains inexplicable—or only explicable within the same colonial narrative construction as *Jane Eyre.* The underside of that violence is the narrative of mutual love, of filial love as operating outside of violence. *Wide Sargasso Sea* also has Black figures (as opposed to people) who populate the text, as crowd or townsfolk, whose actions and movements and whisperings are surreptitious, belligerent, without explanation and therefore purely malevolent (malevolent as opposed to rebellious or desirous of taking and making freedom). *Wide Sargasso Sea* is told in two voices, Antoinette's and Rochester's, but there could just as easily have been three voices. And I find the lack of a third voice structurally unaccountable—except for its colonial logic.

If one is a reader like me, one notices these things. One wants to embrace completely *Wide Sargasso Sea*—strangely, just as this same reader wanted to embrace *Jane Eyre*, and had. Such a reader ignores the misgivings, or rather she reads with a set of aches, forming calluses at each reading. Such a reader has a mindbox inside of a mindbox inside of a mindbox, and so on. And in these boxes are structures of colonial feeling and experience that must be parsed. Such a reader is simultaneously, and some would say clinically, alert to the contradictory recitation. The abject location is a convention of colonial narratives, and one is expected to get used to it in practice also, even as one inhabits it as absurdity and with derision.

Rinaldo Walcott, in his book *The Long Emancipation: Moving Toward Black Freedom*, writes that in European modernity "what it means to be human is continually defined against Black people and blackness. The profound consequences of having humanness defined against Black being means that the project of colonialism and the ongoing workings of coloniality have produced for Black people a perverse relationship to the category of the human. Our existence as human beings remains constantly in question and mostly outside the category of a *life*; it is an existence marked as social death." Despite this, he continues, "social death does not entirely capture the dynamic of life."[43]

At Atocha Train Station in Madrid one recent summer, there is a long line across the reception hall to the ticket purchase counter. My companion and I are standing in the line. Every move we make in the line to the ticket counter is interrupted by white people wishing to cross to the other side of the room. No matter how the line moves, how much closer to the wicket we advance, we are located and used, by white people crossing the hall, as the sign for space. Our physical presence is judged as a void. Our existence, the physical space we occupy, is mapped as a passage through the hall. No matter how we position ourselves—even when we turn our backs to the oncoming person or couple, they press on us; if we stand close to our neighbours, white people try to edge through sideways. We observe that the white people heading toward us are using us as a vector of their sociality. We see this with pique at first, then with anger, and then with philosophical bitterness. We decide that no one will pass through us, and we are bumped or stumbled on with sudden surprise. And we persist. We insist on the "dynamic of life" or we insist on the "category of life." The everyday mundane act of purchasing a train ticket becomes a site of tense contestation of the human. This incident is a common spatial belligerence experienced by Black people at train stations, shops, bars, and in streets.

If structures of sociality derived from the colonial moment pursue us (paraphrasing Édouard Glissant) and are anathema to our living, and if such structures include narration and narrative style, then a rethinking of these forms of address is not only necessary—but urgent, as urgent as the overturning of that sociality.

IV. who is and is not

In *Jane Eyre*, Mr. Brocklehurst exhorts Miss Temple at Lowood orphanage: "Oh, madam, when you put bread and cheese, instead of burnt porridge, into these children's mouths, you may indeed feed their vile bodies, but you little think how you starve their immortal souls!"[44] This is reminiscent of the doctrine of all my primary school teachers, beginning in Miss Greenidge's Dame School when I was three years old. It strikes me that my teachers may have read and lived by this doctrine, and even though I was not in an orphanage, I was one of those children in the great storeroom / training school of British imperialism.

The girl in the photograph—who is and is not me, who is and is not the reader—is still making the photograph. Her sisters and her cousin around her are also making their own photographs, despite her earlier assumption that it is she who is most active in the photograph. That is the beauty of a photograph. Each person may compose their own autobiographies. The succeeding hours outside the photography studio still have not happened—*Vanity Fair* has not been read; *Jane Eyre* has not been read. The tensions in the photograph, the set of colonial and other relations that bring everyone into the studio, may also be arranged toward or in another narrative. The photograph is *previous*. And it is also in the middle of events. Further, it anticipates events. The moment of the photograph is full of in-between-ness as much as it is full of address. It is 1956/57 and much is ahead for the figures inside and outside of the frame. There are social and political movements in progress, precipitated by the histories and tensions of the photograph and its making. C.L.R. James has already written

The Black Jacobins. Eric Williams has already written *Capitalism and Slavery.* The girls in the photograph will arrive home after this public duty is performed. They will give an account to their grandmother of their behaviour at the studio. They will change and put away their good clothes that the photograph required. They've heard of Williams and James somewhat vaguely. They've heard, though not registered, the names; three of them are too young to pay that kind of attention. These names may have been heard in the same breath as "Come, comb your hair" or "Do not go outside." These directives are more important than those names, and the names melt into the commands. Williams and James have been away, too. Though Williams has returned, and there is a hush and excitement when he speaks on the radio in the living room, and his voice is an interruption from play and a signal to go to sleep and be quiet so that the adults may listen.

The frame of the photograph, which one must adjust to or refuse, much like an autobiography, is only becoming present; but the tensions of the frame suggest a small resistance, if not by the girl who is alleged to be me, then to the autobiography of the composed subject. The disarray of the participants, their permeability and liminality, which are the only possessions they have at the moment of taking the photograph—their nothing-yet future and their still-unknown (to themselves) past—all this can still become.

The girl who is supposed to be me is insisting on a photograph, an autobiography of some kind. She does not yet understand (but maybe she glimpses) the full-on violence of narrative. She is trying to be, to centre the girls in the photograph, to find the new medium.

Their brutal fantasies, our realism

I. violent elisions

Scholar, photographer and artist Kevin Adonis Browne's *Hinges, Latches, Locks: Roseau* includes images of rusted old locks, hinges and latches against doorways and containments, edged, sometimes, in galvanized steel. The wood that these metalworks are attached to is deeply worn, painted over and weathered, weathered and painted over. The metal of the nails and latches and hinges and locks is ferrous red and brown, fragile yet forbidding, tentative yet definite in its original purpose. The atmospheres of oxygen and water, acting over a long time, seem to have compounded the seals, stiffened them. Now these works are something other than, or something more than, themselves.

What lies behind these latches and locks? I wonder. Whatever it is, it has been there a long time. Time enough to be irrelevant, surely. Or perhaps time enough to become even more important, since nothing has destroyed the locks and latches and hinges, only deranged them, only made their importance grow the more fragile they've become. Whatever is there remains sealed behind these deceptively weathered latches and locks.

The hinges, hanging on, speak to the once precious or powerful or potent effects or uses of what lies behind them.

The photographer has captured the almost-beauty of the hinges, latches and locks; their hanging on against time. In his essay about these photographs, Browne writes, "In the peeling paint, the rusted mesh, there was your shipwreck and your sugar. Your history in broken hinges. I wonder what is a locked door to a passerby who knows better than to go in?"[45] Browne's essay is perhaps about love, about that particular love that is witness to the other life, the everyday life that accompanies the observation of empire—when one notices simultaneously the life called away from, and the life going on against, empire's drift.

In *A History of Bombing* by the Swedish writer Sven Lindqvist, there is a chapter (or a set of episodes) called "The History of the Future," in which Lindqvist traces, through literature of the late nineteenth and early twentieth centuries (written mostly in English), the emergence/science/evolution of aerial bombing and its imagined uses. In the futurist works of writers William Hay, Samuel W. Odell, Stanley Waterloo, Garrett P. Serviss, Robert W. Cole, Matthew Shiel and Jack London, Lindqvist points out what he calls the "fantasies of genocide" lying "in wait for the first airplanes to arrive." In these fantasies, the era of flight was imagined as the opportunity to use the bomb on non-white populations. As Lindqvist says, "The dream of solving all the problems of the world through mass destruction from the air was already in place before the first bomb was dropped."[46] The plots of all these Euro-fantasies of the time were animated by the subjugation of Africa and India, and elimination of China or all of the "inferior races."

To my mind, these futuristic works are a continuation of the racial imaginary of late seventeenth-, eighteenth- and nineteenth-century works of literature by writers like Aphra Behn, Daniel Defoe, William Thackery, Jane Austen and Emily, Anne and Charlotte Brontë. Those earlier works and their subjects fore-grounded individualism, middle-class making, religiosity and industry—which were, no doubt, their concerns but were also the patina over the colonization/education/eradication/exploitation of the "savages." Giving these works the imprimatur of great literature indemnified the violence of the bourgeoisie. It couched the extreme violence of chattel slavery, colonization and genocide in what was purportedly benign, in the affects of good manners, proper decorum, high graces, great balls, great passions, great ambition; and it granted licence to ignore those events (in the name of good taste). But in these works you might find, if you read well and closely, the "great historical moments" against which these seemingly domestic dramas took place, and the studied innocence of the deep violence that eradicated populations of Indigenous peoples, that murdered and enslaved millions, that immiserated continents and made fortunes. By the time more openly genocidal works of literature appeared, the veneer had been removed and the opportunity for more efficient violence was at hand. The nakedly rabid and xenophobic 1898 Samuel W. Odell novel *The Last War, or the Triumph of the English Tongue* (as pointed out by Lindqvist) may not, at first glance, seem related to Daniel Defoe's 1719 *The Life and Adventures of Robinson Crusoe*—but then, it depends on whose first glance.

I was taught to read those books by Behn, Defoe, Thackery, et al. by passing over the words, by passing over, eliding and skirting the sweep of history in which they lay, and which animated them. And animated me too, with uneasiness.

We were trained *in* reading, and trained *to* read, those seventeenth-, eighteenth- and nineteenth-century literary texts. These texts had, and have, a pedagogical function in colonial and imperialist practices. These fictions were the not-so-soft legitimating apparatus of colonialism and imperialism across many subordinated territories and peoples. These fictions became canonical, they achieved a kind of untouchable status, and they are now attended by acres of criticism which somehow, nevertheless, leaves intact that untouchable status. While the category of fiction avoids being collapsed into the idea of function—by which I mean the idea that fiction does this or that work, or operates in this or that way, or is deployed to this or that effect—the novels and proto-novels that I discuss and gesture to here do have a weight and force in the world. We were trained to read the books, but not to understand the words and their larger contexts.

And of course, again, who is "we"? I think of my university years, for example, as years of sitting in someone else's elisions, someone else's design for the world. An uncomfortable body shifting in its seat, being absorbed into, and absorbing, the toxins of the readings, yet alert to the world in another life.

I have yet another photograph of this reading subject—and it is one where the figure in the photograph is, in fact, me. It is a me that I recognize, and a "me" that still surprises. This time, the figure is not facing the camera but is taken in mid-conversation with another figure. The figures are outside a building. This I recognize, too, as a library on a university campus. Both figures display the same aesthetic, which is markedly different from that earlier photograph, not only because that earlier one was taken in childhood and therefore without the agency of this one but also because this photograph is the antithesis of that tenuously suppliant one. All the energies of dress and action in this photograph declare a purpose quite the opposite of the little girl's in the other, earlier one. I am nineteen or so, in mid-speech, dressed in a tight denim jacket and plaid bell-bottomed pants, hair in a wide Afro, two hands on the hips, one unseen; I am wearing wiry glasses, with a huge green bag on the ground. The bag contains books. The other figure in the photo is a friend, mini-skirted, book in hand. We seem to be talking at the same time. We are obviously discussing something important about political organizing—the Cold War, or Angola. Or something profound about the books we are reading outside of the ones in that library. She is doing economics; I, literature and philosophy, in that moment. But outside of the classrooms we must enter, we are reading the journals *Race Today* and *Freedomways* and books by Frantz Fanon and Eric Williams. This extramural reading will go on throughout our university years, so insufficient is the classroom for what we need to live.

My friend and I are both animated in the photograph; whatever the conversation was, the photograph has registered its intensity. We look as if we are in action, moving, though we are standing still. We look as if whatever we must do is certain and contentious. We are making some arrangement for later, for after class, for this evening, when we will meet again on St. George Street, or in a noisy room full of argument and laughter. Or we are discussing with dismay the everyday verbal assaults we receive in classrooms—the throwaway language, the self-indulgent ignorance our presence elicits from classmates and professors alike. Perhaps what this photograph registers is not so different from what registers in the childhood one. My friend and I have two objectives, running simultaneously. The first is the political urgency outside the library. It is 1973 or 1975—the Black Power movement, the anti-apartheid and liberation struggles are in full flight. We are involved. The second objective is what takes us into the classrooms to secure a BA as an insurance against precarity. This latter objective we have inherited from earlier photographs sent abroad. Now *we* are abroad, as in "foreign," as in away. We leave each other, and we sit in those classrooms of insurances against poverty. The political world is the world of our hopes to overturn the lives of waiting in the first photograph; it is the world of our hopes of overturning all the relations there. The earlier photograph's disarray, the children's permeability, is gradually transforming into knowledge and awareness. We know more than we did then. What might have begun in instinct is coming into view. It is as if the child's rattle has turned into the green bag with all the books; and the sisters and cousin have materialized into the friend—after I followed my big sister, that tall, composed girl, into the university and into the streets of anti-imperialist protests.

When I leave my friend, when I pick up my bag (I remember loving that bag) and disappear into a classroom, it is either seventeenth-, or eighteenth-, or nineteenth-century English literature that I am attending to. These courses are requisite for an undergraduate degree. The professors will make no reference to the histories that produced and buttressed this literature. Those will be dealt with by ignoring them, or through the laissez-faire position of assuming a natural state. Nor will these professors observe the language in the texts that reference these histories and psychologies. Like mine in the classroom, the Black bodies that appear in the novels will be inanimate.

Consistently in those (white) fictions I studied, the "civilized" were the ones addressed, while the "uncivilized" were the ones who bore that signification inside and outside of the text—and were marked as uncivilized despite any alacrity with learning or adoption of the stances of the "civilized." The text, in other words, required that positioning, and designated that positioning as ours. The text/fiction/novel was a template for this most enduring and necessary dyad—the civilized and the savage. The proliferation and standardization of literature and learning (by which I mean, what was to be read, what was to be taught, what was to be learned; and what was not to be read, what was not to be taught, what must not be learned) speaks to the insistence and necessity of this dyad. Whether crudely sophisticated or crudely crude, this formulation of the civilized and the savage accompanied or troubled every text. I received those seventeenth-, eighteenth- and nineteenth-century novels (or pieces of them) first as a child and then as an adult, as lesson and meta-lesson about piety, about obligation, about economy, about how privilege is gained and lost, and about the place that I, and those like me, occupied. Those who stood outside the address were positioned to desire entry, but that entrance would have to be accomplished by self-immolation.

The conviction that other people were to be subjugated for their own good buttressed the seventeenth-, eighteenth- and nineteenth-century novel. Mine is not an argument about being "absent" from literary texts; we were not absent. We were in the texts. Potent as life. But we (and others) were trained to remove or skirt our presence, or to observe that presence as something like background, immutable, not subject to the action of the text. We were like a young Albert (Chinua) Achebe reading *Heart of Darkness* and mistaking himself for the people on the boat and not the grotesque shadowy figures on the shore.

Given the deep influence of it, one might ask: Does this dyad still accompany the novel now? Is it still the latch and hinge of the structure?

II: *Oroonoko* and the racial romantic

Of the seventeenth-century writer Aphra Behn, Virginia Woolf remarked, in *A Room of One's Own*, "All women together ought to let flowers fall upon the tomb of Aphra Behn which is, most scandalously but rather appropriately, in Westminster Abbey, for it was she who earned them the right to speak their minds."[47] Behn is hailed as a protofeminist on the basis of her considerable biography, her fiction, her political writings, and on her position as a white woman in seventeenth-century England struggling to make a living by writing.

Woolf focused on Behn's feats of survival within the framework of a British writing establishment centred in patriarchy and the dominance of male writers and male opinion. But if we look deeper, beyond the fact of the writing to its substance, we might find little difference between Aphra Behn's words and the binary of the civilized and the savage, and the expressions of empire, in the male texts. Some writers and critics contend that Behn's *Oroonoko* was an anti-slavery novel. And in the eighteenth and early nineteenth centuries, as calls for the abolition of slavery grew, the novel was hailed as the first such novel.

Hardly.

There is no doubt that Behn's work in general is formative to the development of the English novel. I recall the first feminist literature courses at the University of Toronto in the late seventies rightly positioning her in that history. It was a time of rehabilitation of women writers, women artists, women scientists, etc.—rehabilitation from patriarchal history. Any contradictions were inconvenient or thought to be bearable in the bourgeois feminist project. Always, the racial hovers in these classrooms; and even in those places with the most radical intentions, racial pedagogy is in attendance. These are the classrooms I attended; and every page I read was, for me, alive with history's immediacies. Yet to be in those rooms felt like wading through stagnant air. Outside, what we called the revolution was in motion; inside was the sedimentation of colonial thought.

Aphra Behn published *Oroonoko, or The Royal Slave* in 1688. It is the story of the enslaved Oroonoko who, before being captured, had been a prince in the region now called Ghana. The novel reflects Behn's travel to Suriname in 1668, the Dutch and English tensions she found there, and her firsthand witnessing of slavery. *Oroonoko*'s white woman narrator comments on the types of colonists and the relations between enslavement and the daily life of settlers. The novel exceeds the realm of fiction, if one understands "fiction" to mean pure invention unrelated to life or something called fact. Behn's book prototypifies the racial romantic genre of novels, cinema, plays—a robust form and a necessary form, for it has its important purposes and uses in the material world of capital and white supremacy. And that genre perhaps begins with *Oroonoko*.

The racial romantic is a set of ideas that seeks to rehabilitate the essentialist categories of race, to prove they are simultaneously true and not true, but nevertheless to keep those ideas fixed; it also seeks to show the extraordinary effort it takes to enter the category of whiteness, and the ultimate sacrifice of doing so. Romantic racism or romantic racialism (a term coined by George Fredrickson) is the ascription of "positive" stereotypes to a group of people in which their difference (from white people) is valorized instead of pathologized. In the case of Behn's *Oroonoko*, this difference is both valorized and pathologized. I will also say that the racial romantic is a site of "illicit" white pleasure, and desire.

Behn's narrator is a woman who travels to/lives in Suriname. She is a wealthy white woman from a wealthy family well connected to the aristocracy. The novella consists of her observations, and in particular her observations about the extraordinary Prince Oroonoko, who is Black and therefore enslaveable, but also not Black, since he must activate the categories of romance, of honour, of fascination, of titillation, of bravery and sacrifice. We enter the work through Behn's descriptions of the relations among people who are Indigenous and white, Black and white. The Black people are enslaved, transported to Suriname and the surrounding region, and the narrator makes the following distinction between Black people (who are not Indigenous) and Indigenous people (who are not Black):

> But before I give you the story of this gallant slave, 'tis fit I tell you the manner of bringing them to these new colonies; those they make use of there not being natives of the place: for those we live with in perfect amity, without daring to command 'em; but, on the contrary, caress 'em with all the brotherly and friendly affection in the world . . . for they have all that is called beauty, except the color, which is a reddish yellow. . . . With these people, as I said, we live in perfect tranquillity and good

understanding, as it behoves us to do; they knowing all the places where to seek the best food of the country, and the means of getting it; and for very small and unvaluable trifles, supply us with what 'tis impossible for us to get: for they do not only in the woods, and over the savannahs, in hunting, supply the parts of hounds, by swiftly scouring through those almost impassable places, and by the mere activity of their feet run down the nimblest deer and other eatable beasts.[48]

The enduring representations of Indigenous peoples of the Americas as amenable to conquest, idealized within nature, living in harmony with colonists, yet of course lacking because they are not white, are all here. The romance of an Edenic space filled with docile "natives" living in a state of nature shapes Behn's narrative. We read, "Religion would here but destroy that tranquillity they possess by ignorance; and laws would but teach 'em to know offense of which they have no notion."[49]

This is the romantic racialism that Behn's writing gifts to narratives that come after it, well into our present time. While the words "perfect tranquillity and good understanding" do not obfuscate that such a state "behoves" those who depend upon Indigenous people's knowledge for their survival, what is hidden, of course, are the expropriations, the massacres, the immiseration of, and the fierce resistances by, the Kalina, the Warao and the Arawak people of the region. Still, the Indigenous are to be distinguished from the Africans transported to the Americas, whose purposes are made clear. We read, "Those then whom we make use of to work in our plantations of sugar are negroes, black slaves altogether, who are transported thither."

But among those Black enslaved is Behn's protagonist Oroonoko—and here arises the case for the special "negro" / the whitened Black. This is the only appearance/visage of an African that might assuage white fears. Oroonoko "was adorned with a native beauty, so transcending all those of his gloomy race that he struck an awe and reverence even into those that knew not his quality . . . who beheld him with surprise and wonder, when afterwards he arrived in our world."[50] This insistence that Oroonoko was not like the other Africans who were enslaved persists throughout the novel. He cannot look like the others. "His face was not of that brown rusty black which most of that nation are, but of perfect ebony, or polished jet."[51] He was really a white man dressed in "ebony."

Behn's narrator proceeds to tell how Oroonoko comes to be a slave in the New World, tracing his lineage as a prince, his gallantry, his perspicacity, his specialness, all of which lift him above the masses of enslaved who did not warrant consideration of their humanity. Naturally, we find that Oroonoko had been taught by a European, further making him special.

> Some part of it we may attribute to the care of a French-
> man of wit and learning, who, finding it turn to very
> good account to be a sort of royal tutor to this young
> black, and perceiving him very ready, apt, and quick of
> apprehension, took a great pleasure to teach him morals,
> language, and science; and was for it extremely beloved

and valued by him. Another reason was, he loved when he came from war, to see all the English gentlemen that traded thither; and did not only learn their language, but that of the Spaniard also, with whom he traded afterwards for slaves. I have often seen and conversed with this great man, and been a witness to many of his mighty actions; and do assure my reader, the most illustrious courts could not have produced a braver man, both for greatness of courage and mind, a judgment more solid, a wit more quick, and a conversation more sweet and diverting. He knew almost as much as if he had read much: he had heard of and admired the Romans: he had heard of the late Civil Wars in England, and the deplorable death of our great monarch; and would discourse of it with all the sense and abhorrence of the injustice imaginable. He had an extreme good and graceful mien, and all the civility of a well-bred great man. He had nothing of barbarity in his nature, but in all points addressed himself as if his education had been in some European court.[52]

Having assured the English reader of the distinction they could make between the shiploads of enslaved and this special one; having whitewashed the body, albeit in ebony, of this one man to produce feeling and empathy and desire in the reader; having declared that but for his colour he would be white, and that only whiteness and its adjacency may produce such feeling and desire—the body cannot yet be totally rid of its blackness. So that blackness becomes a wonder, a magic, an element which remains as a kind of lust. It is this element that Behn and her narrator continue to work in throughout the novel. (The narrator will proceed to do the same for Imoinda, the lover of Oroonoko, who is also sold into slavery.)

The dreadful taxonomies and faux ethnographies of physical and mental attributes, and the ways and habits of Africans and Indigenous people, are so copiously distributed throughout that I would have to quote the book in its entirety to illustrate. But this was the kind of "work" being done at the time of writing: the codification and classification of people from continental "Africa," the Americas and Europe. And these codifications subtend the novel as affect, then become characterization—become, I think, formal literary devices. As in: How do you write a character? How do you describe a person? How do you write a person? Therefore, what is a character? What is a person? What attributes do you give them? This is how the middle-class person becomes the formal subject—and the attempts to become that middle-class person become the subject of the novel. Which is to say, as well, that the novel, the fiction, contains and transports all of these pseudo-ethnographies, these codifications, to readers; it naturalizes them, as much as do journals, diaries and other non-fiction writings of the time. The question is: In what ideological framework do those descriptions live?

In Ghana, Oroonoko is a prince and a slave trader. He has many dealings with French, Spanish and English slave traders until he, along with his whole retinue, is captured through a ruse, sold into slavery by a French slave trader and taken to Suriname. But before his arrival in Suriname, while on board the ship, he embarks on a hunger strike, and the captain, in order to stop it, promises to free him as soon as they touch land. Oroonoko then persuades his retinue of the honesty of the captain. Naturally, none of what is promised comes to pass; the prince and his retinue remain enslaved. But what the novel establishes in this moment is Oroonoko's undying faith in European affectations of honesty, integrity, fealty. These ideological markers of sociality will drive the English novel, or rather the bourgeois novel, through several centuries—they are the meta-discourse in an age of massive proximate violence, even as the actions in and of the texts belie the discourse and the age. The violence, as represented in these texts, is already assigned a civilizing exemption; and, in these texts, the action that is or will be violence is lost from sight. (Think forward to that moment in *Jane Eyre* when Jane refuses St. John's proposal of marriage and offers, instead, to accompany him as "a sister." And where is St. John going? To India to take up his missionary/colonizing work.) The actions of love, betrayal, ambition, honour, necessity, the labour of rags to riches, the draw of charm—these emerge as the primary subjects of these works. The scrim of propriety, grace and valour marks the great elision of colonial violence—the ongoing murders, massacres, large-scale abductions and genocides. Brutal social rending is, in this way, elided in the literary. These are the elisions, someone else's, that my friend and I endured inside the university classrooms. They are implied by the green bag of books in the photograph where I recognize my younger self.

In *Oroonoko* we read,

> They sold 'em off, as slaves, to several merchants and gentlemen; not putting any two in one lot, because they would separate 'em far from each other; nor daring to

trust 'em together, lest rage and courage should put 'em upon contriving some great action, to the ruin of the colony. . . . The gentleman that bought him was a young Cornish gentleman whose name was Trefry; a man of great wit and fine learning, and was carried into those parts by the Lord Governor to manage all his affairs. He, reflecting on the last words of Oroonoko to the captain, and beholding the richness of his vest, no sooner came into the boat but he fixed his eyes on him; and finding something so extraordinary in his face, his shape and mien, a greatness of look, and haughtiness in his air, and finding he spoke English, had a great mind to be inquiring into his quality and fortune: which, though Oroonoko endeavored to hide, by only confessing he was above the rank of common slaves, Trefry soon found he was yet something greater than he confessed; and from that moment began to conceive so vast an esteem for him that he ever after loved him as his dearest brother, and showed him all the civilities due to so great a man.[53]

Here is the deletion that obfuscates the violence, the inhumane. To say that the "gentleman" who bought Oroonoko is of "fine wit" is to surround the verb "bought" and the object "him" with the subject "gentlemen" and the adjectival "fine wit"; it is to move the descriptor (which is slavery) so far away, to bury it so deep that it is indistinguishable, illegible, unintelligible. The life foregrounded, and the desire to aestheticize white life, European life, entangles certain affects and relations of power—such as slave owning—with refinement of character and taste. So too is

the folding of ownership, a relation of dominance and subjugation, into feelings of "love" accomplished narratively, not unlike
how other forms of servitude and oppression are wrapped in
paternalism. What sly obscuring.

And one must ask: How is any of what is described in the
quote above possible?

Oroonoko is sold into slavery by the same Europeans who
buy from him, and who, according to Behn's narrator, he adores.
After he is purchased, we are told that he is awarded pride of
place among the enslaved, treated like a prince and an "equal" to
the whites. Of what is this "equality" made? His status does not
change, and he is assigned the new name Caesar—just as possessions are assigned new names according to their use. Caesar: a
classical name that is both parody of, and insult to, Oroonoko's
situation. Many slave owners of this period and later imposed
this renaming joke on enslaved people; it is another sign of the
delight that Europeans took in the practice of slavery. The man
who buys Oroonoko, and thus renames him, promises him freedom but dies before he grants it.

Significant here is the description of African traders of slaves.
Oroonoko is presented as having the respect of the people whom
he himself earlier traded into slavery. But why would slaves,
upon later meeting the man who traded them, venerate him,
after being captured and sold away from their territories? This
narrative serves to bolster the idea that the enslaved embraced
their lot, were of weak character and intelligence, and were therefore properly assigned to their place. One thinks of the 1734
account of the life of Ayuba Suleiman Diallo—called "Job ben
Solomon"—recorded by Thomas Bluett, and Diallo's portrait,

which was painted by William Hoare in 1733. Diallo had been a slave trader from what is now called Senegal. He was then captured himself and transported to the colony of Maryland in what becomes the United States. By reason of his resistance and coming to the attention of people who marvelled at his literacy, Muslim faith and class status, his freedom was purchased and he was sent to London, after which he made his way back to Senegal. This narrative of an elite class of "African" must have fascinated eighteenth-century Europe, and the portrait of Diallo by Hoare is mercifully missing caricature of the type so redolent of the period.

It is hardly likely that people who had been sold by Behn's character Oroonoko—or by Diallo—would have greeted him on the other side with anything but hatred and contempt, but this is another romantic trope of capital: that oppressed (Black) people love their oppressors.

The fantasies of oppression and violence range across multiple relations of class, sex and race power. These fantasies are necessary to the maintenance and sustenance of such relations in the sense that they are the verbal or written articulations of those relations; they mythologize and justify the brutalities; they use language, the terrain of meaning, to territorialize meaning, interpretation, existence. They are as necessary as the violence. If conquest, slavery and colonization of lands and people are the main aim, mythologizing and control of the imagination are the equally important conduit to this end. And in Behn's *Oroonoko* these fantasies, these mythologies, are plentiful and thorough.

75

Behn is working in the ideas of her era. She is creating stories that narrativize the life of the period. More, she is writing work that constitutes the life of the period and then imagines it into time—past, present, future.

A novel is an artifact of its time. We ascribe to it a distance called "art," and we equivocate along the line of that distance. "European art" (in this instance something called "the novel") seals the form against indictments of its very narration of that time. In this way, it is simultaneously sealing and revealing the affective economies' adjacent position to the political economy. One might say that the affective is the way that the political economy circulates. That is, the political economy is conjoined with the affective, conjoined with desires; and the relations of ruling inhabit the affective.

> And he was received more like a governor than a slave . . .
> assigned him his portion of land, his house, and his busi-
> ness up in the plantation. But as it was more for form
> than any design to put him to his task, he endured no
> more of the slave but the name, and remained some days
> in the house, receiving all visits that were made him, with-
> out stirring towards that part of the plantation where the
> negroes were. . . . But he no sooner came to the houses
> of the slaves, which are like a little town by itself, the
> negroes all having left work, but they all came forth to
> behold him, and found he was that prince who had, at
> several times, sold most of 'em to these parts; and from a
> veneration they pay to great men, especially if they know
> 'em, and from the surprise and awe they had at the sight

of him, they all cast themselves at his feet, crying out,
in their language, "Live, O King! Long live, O King!"
and kissing his feet, paid him even divine homage.[54]

The preposterous idea that Oroonoko was welcomed as a governor is sheer fantasy, a fantasy to further differentiate him from
the "negroes." It is a fantasy that further polishes the reputation
and the sensibilities of the colonizer—racist oppressors forgiving
themselves mass human rights crimes but elevating the singular
worthy among the Black. The text was published in 1688, when
a monarchist discourse, a discourse of aristocracy, is dominant.
But there is also a republican discourse that is no less pernicious.
John Locke is writing his *An Essay Concerning Human Understanding*. It will appear in 1689, one year after *Oroonoko*. Locke
is, of course, an investor in the slave-trading Royal Africa Society,
a secretary of the Council of Trade and Plantations and secretary to the Lords Proprietors of the Carolinas. The enrichening
of the British aristocracy by investments in shipping, the slave
trade and other subsidiary trades is on the surface of the culture.
It is the main organizing principle of economic life, of civic life
and of daily life—it produces not only sugar, cotton and other
products, but also people, their social locations, and the ideas
that underpin, invigorate and maintain those locations. In
Oroonoko we read:

> Trefry, who was naturally amorous, and loved to talk of
> love as well as anybody, proceeded to tell him they had
> the most charming black that ever was beheld on their
> plantation, about fifteen or sixteen years old, as he guessed;

that for his part he had done nothing but sigh for her ever since she came; and that all the white beauties he had seen never charmed him so absolutely as this fine creature had done; and that no man, of any nation, ever beheld her that did not fall in love with her; and that she had all the slaves perpetually at her feet; and the whole country resounded with the fame of Clemene. "For so," said he, "we have christened her: but she denies us all with such a noble disdain that 'tis a miracle to see that she who can give such eternal desires should herself be all ice and unconcern. She is adorned with the most graceful modesty that ever beautified youth; the softest sigher—that, if she were capable of love, one would swear she languished for some absent happy man and so retired as if she feared a rape ..."[55]

This whole paragraph qualifies as parody. By means of literary coincidence, Imoinda, the love of Oroonoko's life before enslavement, has also been enslaved and transported to Suriname, and sold to the same man, Trefy. She is renamed Clemene, after Clymene in Greek mythology, who is, among other things, the mother of Atlas and Prometheus. Trefy describes his encounter and desire for her to Oroonoko, and two fantasies collapse into one. The complete romanticization and whitewashed narrativization of rape proceeds, as do the fantasies that a slave could exert will and give consent. The subordinated and "rape-able" condition of African/Black women in slavery is not news, now or then. But this presentation of choice as a possibility for Imoinda does disingenuous work. Imoinda is enslaved but the narrator "manages" both the violence of slavery and the violence of rape by suggesting that choice, consent and "free will" can be expressed by an enslaved woman. Here is the patriarchal myth of the woman withholding; and here is the occluding and masking of the "ownership" of Imoinda by Trefys—the masking of the fact that to be a slave is to be subject in all ways to the will of those who claim ownership over you. The pretense of the writing normalizes and aestheticizes violence. Terror and anxiety are called "ice" and "unconcern."

Amazingly the word "rape" appears in the paragraph—but in this way: . . . *and so retired as if she feared a rape.* I am sure that she feared rape. Indeed, by now she would have been raped. Rape, not called rape, was part of the quotidian violence faced by Black women who were enslaved. Behn places the word here in another elision: "as if" is doing the same distancing and obfuscating work as that earlier "gentleman," "fine wit" and "bought." And there is that curious prepositional phrase, "if she were capable of love."

Trefy says, "I have been ready to make use of those advantages of strength and force nature has given me: but oh! she disarms me with that modesty . . ." In other words, Trefy declares that he would in fact rape Imoinda except for her "modesty." This in a conversation with Oroonoko, who does not yet know that Imoinda is the woman referred to; and he concurs with Trefy. Here the author provides the masculinist similarity between the two men in this discourse on Imoinda/Clemene as well as the vaunted decency of white society and its gallant masculinity. Weeping, she is "'so tender and so moving that I retire, and thank my stars she overcame me.' The company laughed at his civility to a slave."[56]

No doubt knowing full well what the everyday life of some-one enslaved was like, and especially an enslaved woman, the company probably laughed at Trefy's mendacity. Or, having also committed such violence, the company laughed at this inside joke. But here we might note the contradiction in the produc-tion of white masculinity at this time: it offered white men a veneer of civility over the constant use of deep violence. What is white masculinity, we might ask? What does it consist of, dis-cursively and otherwise?

The novel is full of answers to these questions through its normalizing of hierarchy, disappearing of conflict and regular-izing of the state of affairs into a flat, seamless, taken-for-granted world. At the same time, it gestures to—no, it encourages—a certain aesthetic pleasure in violence. Take this sentence ending the near-rape story: "Thus passed they this night, after having received from the slaves all imaginable respect and obedience."[57] I rather think that the night would have been spent in great unease, rage, resentment and fear at the memory of rape for many of the enslaved listening. The watchers and the listeners who are enslaved in the story are produced as passive backdrop to the construction of a white discourse that in every way folds their brutalization into pleasure. They are privy to and observers of the metastasis of language itself—or rather, its metathesis.

Behn's novel is awash in the politics of the times. The narrator tells her tale with a kind of joy—with drama, pathos, ornate and high tone and language, detail of events, feeling and description of landscape—to an audience curious for such things. But when we read this, we cannot merely read it as if it is above the fray of the political, the way that one is overwhelmingly urged to read "art" (a contentious category, as it seeks to disengage with the very processes it describes), detaching the novel from its time—or precisely because of the passage of time, assigning it a value-free (and at the same time, valued) status. Writers and readers didn't do that work then, and we can't now. We must read the novel as being engaged with its time vigorously, as text proselytizing that time.

Here is a passage:

> About this time we were in many mortal fears about some disputes the English had with the Indians; so that we could scarce trust ourselves, without great numbers, to go to any Indian towns or place where they abode, for fear they should fall upon us, as they did immediately after my coming away; and the place being in the possession of the Dutch, they used them not so civilly as the English: so that they cut in pieces all they could take, getting into houses, and hanging up the mother and all her children about her; and cut a footman, I left behind me, all in joints, and nailed him to trees.[58]

Earlier descriptions of Indigenous peoples as accommodating, friendly and docile are contradictorily expressed throughout the novel; one must focus to keep up with them, to keep clear in the face of them. And when we focus, we learn that in fact the colonists live in mortal fear of the people whose territory they usurped. "For my part, I took 'em for hobgoblins, or fiends, rather than men," the narrator says, "but however their shapes appeared, their souls were very humane and noble." In the passage quoted above, the narrator seeks to put the blame for this conflict on the Dutch. She makes distinctions between Dutch and English rule and forms of barbarity. We learn of contentious and competitive relations among colonizing powers who use and cast each other as more or less brutal. But this compels a reader like me to understand that the regime of violence is the given; and while accusations as to which colonial state is lesser or more barbarous might be the weapons of propaganda each throws against the other, these should not distract us from the fact that slavery is barbarity, that colonization is barbarity.

Despite his own lack of freedom, Oroonoko, oddly, becomes protector and conduit of the English whites against the Indigenous people. And when the narrator and other colonists go among the Indigenous villages, Oroonoko miraculously turns into an interpreter, and then morphs into a white avatar.

Among the Indigenous peoples in the text, whiteness is what is strange and made to surprise—the spectacle. Meanwhile, the war captains of the villages are described as both "children" and "evil spirits" of "so dreadful a spectacle."[59] Yet, we are told, their souls are human and noble. The speed at which the narrative switches and manufactures plausibility for all the distortions of the "other" in the white imagination is striking and says something about this facility as a persuasive tool in English storytelling. So, where else can we locate this linguistic signal/call/gesture/logic? In the depiction of Oroonoko, who is given the ability to understand this "other" because he is "other" too. It is he who wants to meet the war captains and he who leads the whites through the village. In productions of Behn's *Oroonoko* for stage in the eighteenth century, the novel-turned-play is accompanied by the illustrated work of Henry Fuseli showing a Greek-statue-like Oroonoko leading the fearful whites in an attack against the Indigenous people.

In the end, of course, it is impossible for Oroonoko to survive in this text and in this period (or I might say in any period, since I draw a relation between Oroonoko and figures in the contemporary racial imaginary). And it is also necessary that he be tragic, and a lesson in the impossibility of his existence. Oroonoko rebels because *his* freedom is not given as promised, not because he finds slavery abhorrent. He rebels because a personal demand for freedom, a special demand, is reneged on.

Caesar, having singled out these men from the women and children, made an harangue to 'em, of the miseries and ignominies of slavery; counting up all their toils and sufferings, under such loads, burdens, and drudgeries as were fitter for beasts than men; senseless brutes, than human souls. He told 'em it was not for days, months, or years, but for eternity; there was no end to be of their misfortunes: they suffered not like men who might find a glory and fortitude in oppression; but like dogs, that loved the whip and bell, and fawned the more they were beaten: that they had lost the divine quality of men, and were become insensible asses, fit only to bear; nay, worse; an ass, or dog, or horse, having done his duty could lie down in retreat, and rise to work again, and while he did his duty, endured no stripes; but men, villainous, senseless men, such as they, toiled on all the tedious week till Black Friday: and then, whether they worked or not, whether they were faulty or meriting, they, promiscuously, the innocent with the guilty, suffered the infamous whip, the sordid stripes, from their fellow-slaves, till their blood trickled from all parts of their body; blood, whose every drop ought to be revenged with a life of some of those tyrants that impose it. "And why," said he, "my dear friends and fellow-sufferers, should we be slaves to an unknown people? Have they vanquished us nobly in fight? Have they won us in honorable battle? And are we by the chance of war become their slaves? This would not anger a noble heart; this would not animate a soldier's soul: no, but we are bought and sold like apes or monkeys, to be the sport of women, fools, and cowards; and the support of rogues and runagates, that have abandoned their own countries for rapine, murders, theft, and villainies. Do you not hear every day how they upbraid each other with infamy of life, below the wildest savages? And shall we render obedience to such a degenerate race, who have no one human virtue left, to distinguish them from the vilest creatures? Will you, I say, suffer the lash from such hands?" They all replied with one accord, "No, no, no; Caesar has spoke like a great captain, like a great king."[60]

It is probably by way of this anti-slavery speech of Oroonoko's that the novel later gained attention as an anti-slavery work. Likely, too, this reputation was helped by the novel's subsequent production on stage in the late eighteenth century. The argument for emancipation becomes wrapped in the heroic, but only for some, not for all—only for those Blacks who were open to being "educated" out of blackness, or who strove to achieve approval from whiteness. This was a very specific genre of "deserving" that did not undercut the definition of savages even as it sought to elevate the worthy and to make a case for another kind of proximate, incomplete freedom—namely emancipation. This term described a gradual freeing, one which attributed a half-human-until-educated status to the enslaved. And if the play *Oroonoko* fueled abolitionist ideas in the eighteenth century, it was contained in the idea of the exceptional negro who would be of assistance to whiteness and imperialism—the exceptional negro who would be the hero.

Those of us reading who in some way identify with Oroonoko, however badly he is represented as "ourselves," know what the outcome of his rebellion will be. And we are thrown into sadness at the coming disappointment—the imminent failure of this act of rebellion; in fact, the inevitable failure which will in time be represented as failure of character. We are disappointed here, even as we wish this fictional rebellion to work; but we know of thousands of rebellions, small and major. It is 1688 and there are two hundred years more of slavery to follow in Suriname, until 1863, and so we are exhausted at the thought. We know that this rebellion will be put down, and that hundreds of years of oppression will proceed. We feel no respite from it; we know no different way of living will be available to this "hero." He is, we are, enclosed by the period in these lives, and enclosed in their echoes. And enclosed too by the racist heroic/romantic versions of us that will play out on stages and in texts for years to come, reaching into these centuries in which we now live.

The denouement of the novel, of course, is the other speech by Oroonoko—the one he gives on the failure of the rebellion, saying that he had tried to make free people of those who were "by nature slaves." This is where the narrator reconciles the difference between her hero and the masses of enslaved people. In this way we may be allowed to dismiss calls for emancipation—and that dismissal may come from the mouth of the good Black, the heroic Black. And by personalizing the demands for freedom, white domination is rescued as a general norm. In other words, the elevation of Oroonoko gives him access to the right to personalize freedom and separate it from a general call to freedom. Added to this, the condemnation of the enslaved as not ambitious enough, not courageous enough, by Oroonoko himself, "one of their own," confirms the original proposition that they were only fit to be slaves. Naturally the rebellion fails, as all rebellions in a white narrative must—because rightness must be restored, goodness of the colonial enterprise asserted. The words that follow may arise out of the slavocracy, but they could well be words arising out of a liberal democracy today, one that situates the protagonists in the same relation to white supremacy: "Caesar was taken and whipped like a common slave. We met on the river with Colonel Martin, a man of great gallantry, wit, and goodness, and whom I have celebrated in a character of my new comedy, by his own name, in memory of so brave a man. He was wise and eloquent, and, from the fineness of his parts, bore a great sway over the hearts of all the colony."[61]

Throughout, the off-kilter description of someone engaged in conquest and enslavement is deployed. Referring to someone as gallant, brave *and* a colonist is an elision of a magnitude of thousands—a white elision, an elision through which all of whiteness is transported, a lacuna in which all of whiteness is encircled and encircles.

> . . . and the executioner came, and first cut off his members, and threw them into the fire; after that, with an ill-favored knife, they cut off his ears and his nose and burned them; he still smoked on, as if nothing had touched him; then they hacked off one of his arms, and still he bore up, and held his pipe; but at the cutting off the other arm, his head sunk, and his pipe dropped, and he gave up the ghost, without a groan or a reproach.[62]

As if everything isn't already horrific enough, the details of Oroonoko's torture after his rebellion exceed all. What work do they do? What objective do they serve? There is prurience and a kind of pleasure in the details here—"and first cut off his members . . ." And because blackness exceeds the human, as Oroonoko is being hacked to death he bears it all while smoking a pipe. He eventually dies without so much as a "groan" or a "reproach." The description is horrific. As Zakiyyah Iman Jackson writes, "black(ened) people are not so much dehumanized as non-humans or cast as liminal humans nor are black(ened) people framed as animal-like or machine-like but are cast as sub, supra, and human *simultaneously* and in a manner that puts being in peril because the operations of simultaneously being everything and nothing for an order—human, animal, machine, for instance—constructs black(ened) humanity as the privation and exorbitance of form."[63]

I began by saying that *Oroonoko* is a novel that plays in the racial romantic. So what is the other half of the romance? Is it this figure who bears all hardship for love of whiteness, even if whiteness disappoints or is brutal? Is it the "slave" who dotes on whiteness and is always working toward its goodness? The "slave" whose nobility is acknowledged, envied, dismissed, seen as different from the savagery of "his own kind," but is never quite enough to exist alongside whiteness—rather, becomes that which whiteness uses as a further note of demarcation? This blackness, whiteness declares, is the kind of blackness that may enter the lifeworld. And this romance must always end in death or demise or in ongoing servitude. This figure must die for its honesty or innocence or its disappointment, its inability to uphold such nobility, or modesty, etc. Or the figure must be proven to be just too good to be true—as opposed to the good-enough "slave."

The racial romantic offers a template for the many representations of Black people—in particular, Black people in positions of power who are supposed to forbear white supremacy's excesses. There are many figures and scenarios that have played out, and still play out, this template across time. Think of Tiger Woods's characterization in the media—his exceptional darling status, and his demise. Think of the visual representations of him, the questions of race, his coining of the word "Cablinasian," his own investment in the trope, and then, after his fall from grace, the appearance of an entirely new Tiger on the cover of *Vanity Fair*: shirtless, darkened, wearing a skull cap, and looking "menacing."[64] Think of Barack Obama, and the many questions that the right raised about his allegiances, the myriad ways that his image and his familial links to the continent of Africa were deployed; think also of how his white mother and grandfather were utilized to bolster his legitimacy.[65] These are but a few examples of this racial romantic imaginary in the contemporary. The characterization of Obama is the characterization of Oroonoko—just as any Black figure who rises to or occupies a position of power in white capital comes to be characterized as Oroonoko in the white imagination. This figure is always being sought—that is, Black men are asked to be this prince (or are positioned against this prince) in the white imagination only to be dismantled when that figure's usefulness is at an end. That is when the narrative, fictional or real, may make full use of the figure's demise—to confirm the uselessness of its entry into existence.

III. or the adventure is always already violent

Daniel Defoe's *The Life and Adventures of Robinson Crusoe* is set in 1651–94, and was published in 1719, thirty-one years after *Oroonoko, or The Royal Slave*. I will not reproduce the plot of *Robinson Crusoe* so much as index some of its possible significations, which so often go unattended in favour of praise for its narrative structure and lasting influence on English novels. The story is known, and one needs only the slightest of gestures to usher its spectre into every room. It has become a compelling template for narrative structure and narrative idea in the novel, for plot and feeling. So: someone goes into the world, an unfamiliar world, where there is no food or shelter and there are hostile elements whose purpose is to kill or capture you. You arm yourself, you find food, you wait for deliverance, you appeal to God. You say, "If I get out of this, I will never do this again." You discover God. You bargain with God. You avoid the hostile non-human life, you kill some of the hostile almost-human life—and you save some of them, who are so grateful that henceforth they adore you. Eventually, you are rescued, and you win the prize.

Oh no, wait: that's a long-running reality TV show, *Survivor*.

One can fill in the countless narratives, the countless iterations of this novel, in the many education and communication regimes of the past and present. Let's go back to 1719, then, and *The Life and Adventures of Robinson Crusoe*.

———

Our expectation at the outset of the novel is the survival of Crusoe. Adventures never end in death—at least, not for the protagonist, and not in novels. They are about life and death, but the protagonist must survive. And we are taken in by that desire and expectation. We wonder: How will he fare? How will he continue to live? We know vaguely that his survival depends on slavery, as this is more than a shadow at the beginning of the text. Perhaps it is somewhere in the warnings and reticence of the father: stay in England, make a living on the secondary and tertiary economies of slave trading and plantation slavery. But the reader is positioned with the protagonist, against his father— longing to defy the father, to experience the world. Crusoe is young and fleeing a dull life and his father's control. We want him to go on the adventure. How else will the book proceed?

The innocence implied, or introduced, in the word "adventure"—the gesture toward the seemingly unknown—is not innocence at all, but a will to strive and to make something. And in the eighteenth and nineteenth centuries, readers understood what that something was, just as we too understand: notions of investment, finances, venture capital, etc. We know the words; we demur the meanings. As those earlier readers did. Or, we love the meanings. As they did.

Crusoe is "entirely bent upon seeing the world."[66] To "see the world" is a working phrase for exploitation; likewise, to go abroad, to make one's fortune, and so on, are all euphemisms or understandings for conquest—or profit, at least. The adventure is already violent—it presupposes an encounter that has no boundaries and from which there will be profit. It is not a "journey" with travellers who go to seek enlightenment; an adventure is not a supplicant act. (And even a journey of "enlightenment" is surely wed to the adventures of slavery and genocide.) The adventure sets out as the character does, a character who indeed may change—but only toward aggression, because he expects to encounter dangers. There is a penetrating quality to the adventure. It is prepared for violence or harm, either receiving or giving that violence. It is prepared to act, as opposed to witness. An aggressive foray is understood in the word "adventure." The landscape of adventure is kinetic, volatile, risky. And the adventurer is prepared for battle.

We read that Crusoe "first got acquainted with the master of a ship who had been on the coast of Guinea; and who, having had very good success there, was resolved to go again. . . . I carried about £40 in such toys and trifles as the captain directed me to buy. These £40 I had mustered together by the assistance of some of my relations whom I corresponded with; and who, I believe, got my father, or at least my mother, to contribute so much as that to my first adventure."[67]

And so, early in the novel, the coast of Guinea appears. "Very good success" is the euphemism, the sign, for slave trading. On that Guinean coast, the toys and trifles will be traded for what is poor, for what is valuable: "in a word, this voyage made me both a sailor and a merchant; for I brought home five pounds nine ounces of gold-dust for my adventure, which yielded me in London, at my return, almost £300; and this filled me with those aspiring thoughts which have since so completed my ruin."[68]

This mathematics signifies the colonial enterprise's profitability, even for one so young. It speaks of the complete immersion of the *material* and the *imaginary* into the economics of slavery, with all its attendant and emerging industries. The unit of coin the *guinea* is minted in Britain around 1663.

Early in the novel, too, on one of these voyages to the continent, Crusoe is captured and himself taken into slavery for two years in what is now called Morocco. When Crusoe is captured and enslaved himself, do we stop? Do we expect him to turn back? No. We are, in other words, aware of the slave trade as we proceed, and so we ignore it, or we think it mere window dressing to, or terrain of his survival. Does Crusoe become enlightened? No. Just as eighteenth- and nineteenth-century readers would have been entirely aware of what "adventure" meant, they also understood what seafaring, what going to the New World meant; what working on ships and what going to sea meant. They were familiar with the world of the novel outside of the novel, which the novel re-presented. And this novel reflected their lives and their aspirations, their desires and perhaps their fears.

After two years enslaved, Crusoe escapes along with a young boy named Xury, who was also enslaved. They sail the west coast of Africa, waiting for rescue. Crusoe knows that "all the ships from Europe"[69] traverse this coast. Chattel slavery is a hustle, a hot market. Defoe writes: "We saw people stand upon the shore to look at us; we could also perceive they were quite black and naked."[70] And so, all along the coast, Crusoe is helped by the black and naked people; he and Xury are given water and food, but he will only view these people as savages.[71] Finally, they encounter a ship. And the "boy" Xury—who has saved him many times, who is never represented as needing his own freedom, who encountered the same difficulties as he along the coast, who was in as much peril as he, and who presumably was also fleeing slavery—Crusoe sells. And he regrets this later only because he acquires a plantation in Brazil that needs labour.

Throughout the narrative it is amazing what is taken for granted, what becomes discursive, what is carried as logic, what is presumed to be normal, what *is* normal—namely, whiteness as represented in humans who may do what they will with "savages," despite affiliation. The protagonist's focus assumes and carries the weight of affinity, and the reader's affinities are assumed, too. The moral weight is with the protagonist, no matter their actions. So: Crusoe buys into the trade and is captured and enslaved, which we are meant to feel is wrong, but only for him. Xury's desires we are not allowed to apprehend. The Black signifier is readily and optimally present for service. But of his own enslavement Crusoe tells us: "And now I was once more delivered from the most miserable of all conditions of life; and what to do next with myself I was to consider."[72] Admittedly, then, slavery is the most miserable of all conditions of life. Yet the answer to what to do next is to submit other people to it.

The book is full of these contradictions—but perhaps they are not contradictions, since the designation of human only applies to Europeans. A Portuguese captain recommends Brazil to Crusoe, and so he is taken there.

> I had not been long here before I was recommended to the house of a good honest man like himself, who had an *ingenio*, as they call it (that is, a plantation and a sugar-house). I lived with him some time, and acquainted

myself by that means with the manner of planting and making of sugar; and seeing how well the planters lived, and how they got rich suddenly, I resolved, if I could get a licence to settle there, I would turn planter among them: resolving in the meantime to find out some way to get my money, which I had left in London, remitted to me.[73]

The protagonist here is plain-speaking about his intentions; the elision is within literature and the literary. Literature has made him an "everyman," an exemplary character whose feat of survival is to be admired and duplicated. We might call this narrator unreliable now—but perhaps only some of us would. A reader like me is alert to the story and finds the narrator abhorrent. A reader like me is wondering about Xury and is broken at this point.

The enterprise of slavery is the constant. It is how fortunes are made, it continues apace, and even taking into consideration within Crusoe's experience on the island later, it is the exciting charge of his life. All the people he meets, whether castaway or abandoned, all the ships run aground, are in this enterprise. In Brazil he is a wealthy landowner with a few slaves and servants. The tales that he regales his fellow planters with are about the lucrativeness of the enterprise of slavery, about how rich the continent is for plunder. And this is the enterprise that leads to Crusoe becoming shipwrecked. He is eager to engage in it—and each time, he makes an account of the monies he has and the possibility of making more.

There is a tone to the telling that says, "Oh, I should have just been happy with what I had, but darn me." Crusoe demurs rhetorically when telling us that he is the architect of his own demise as he pursues what he calls "wandering abroad in search of adventure." The enterprise and the source of adventure is slavery, and the resource-rich African continent and Americas.

> I had frequently given them an account of my two voyages to the coast of Guinea: the manner of trading with the negroes there, and how easy it was to purchase upon the coast, for trifles—such as beads, toys, knives, scissors, hatchets, bits of glass, and the like—not only gold-dust, Guinea grains, elephants' teeth, &c., but negroes, for the service of the Brazils, in great numbers. They listened always very attentively to my discourses on these heads, but especially to that part which related to the buying of negroes, which was a trade at that time, not only not far entered into, but, as far as it was, had been carried on by assientos, or permission of the kings of Spain and Portugal, and engrossed in the public stock: so that few negroes were bought, and these excessively dear.
>
> . . . . and they came to make a secret proposal to me; and, after enjoining me to secrecy, they told me that they had a mind to fit out a ship to go to Guinea; that they had all plantations as well as I, and were straitened for nothing so much as servants; that as it was a trade that could not be carried on, because they could not publicly sell the negroes when they came home, so they desired to make but one voyage, to bring the negroes on shore privately, and divide them among their own plantations; and, in a word, the question was whether I would go their super-cargo in the ship, to manage the Trading Part

upon the coast of Guinea? And they offer'd me that I
should have my equal share of the negroes. . . .[74]

These tales told in the seventeenth and eighteenth centuries are
the foundation not only of storytelling, but also of the cultural
imaginary. And this imaginary echoes forward.

It echoes forward to September 4, 2022 when, days before
she was named British prime minister, Liz Truss declared that
she does not believe in looking through the lens of the "redistribution" of wealth (as quoted in the *Guardian* that same day).
When shown calculations that her planned reversal of a recent
rise in national insurance would benefit top earners by about
£1,800 per year and the lowest earners by about £7 per year, and
asked if this was fair, Truss said: "Yes, it is fair." She continued:
"The people at the top of the income distribution pay more tax,
so inevitably when you cut taxes, you tend to benefit people who
are more likely to pay tax. But to look at everything through the
lens of redistribution, I believe, is wrong. Because what I'm about
is growing the economy. And growing the economy benefits
everybody. So far, the economic debate for the past twenty years
has been dominated by discussions about distribution. But
what's happened is that we have had relatively low growth."[75]

Truss's calculation here is of the same sort as in that earlier
period—by which I mean that Truss is inhabiting an imagination that does not factor in, because it does not see, the extraction
of labour from the poor and indentured as part of any equation
called "wealth." She calls such a factor "redistribution," not bills
or accounts due from exploitation, and thereby dismisses it. The
accounts are always settled as if those on the bottom deserve yet

more exploitation rather than compensation and the cessation of exploitation. We are still living with the brutal mathematics of that colonial time, even as Truss and many other politicians appeal to the supposed moral correctness of their position, a moral "rectitude" that reflects the "true" and "good" order of the world.

One sees this quality in Defoe's novel, rife as it is with religious musings also. These musings, a common device in eighteenth- and nineteenth-century novels, are spread over many pages. Consider this passage:

> . . . beginning at the New Testament, I began seriously to read [the Bible], and imposed upon myself to read a while every morning and every night; not tying myself to the number of chapters, but as long as my thoughts should engage me. It was not long after I set seriously to this work, but I found my heart more deeply and sincerely affected with the wickedness of my past life. I was earnestly begging of God to give me repentance, when it happened providentially, the very day, that, reading the Scripture, I came to these words: "He is exalted a Prince and a Saviour, to give repentance and to give remission." I threw down the book; and with my heart as well as my hands lifted up to heaven, in a kind of ecstasy of joy, I cried out aloud, "Jesus, thou son of David! Jesus, thou exalted Prince and Saviour, give me repentance!"
>
> This was the first time I could say, in the true sense of the words, that I prayed in all my life; for now I prayed with a sense of my condition, and my thoughts being

directed, by a constant reading the Scripture and praying to God, to things of a higher nature, I had a great deal of comfort within, which till now I knew nothing of; also, my health and strength returned.[76]

The telling juxtapositions quoted here never seem to trouble the god of these musings, who sends the supplicants away with blessings and licence to reign over all.

The novels of these centuries defaulted to Christian philosophy as a soporific, an elision of their intentions, an allusion to the power conscripted to them, given by God. This begs a reader like me to say that I am not the sympathetic reader, and that I find this maudlin rather than sorrowful. A reader like me thinks that if "heaven" determined anything, then Crusoe's abandonment on the island is what he deserved—though not what the Indigenous people deserved. A reader like me thinks "Providence" ruined many of his creatures and rendered them miserable by the trade of this protagonist and his ilk. And if one were a reader like me, one would at this point wish for Crusoe's demise. One would want the narrative to end here, where he is at his most bereft. But that would be a reader like me.

If one were not a reader like me, one would yet again experience apprehension or sympathize with the protagonist's fear over his demise. His reprehensible nature would not be repulsive. That reader would not say, "Serves you right." The reader who admires these confessions is easily seduced or is so deep inside the ideological ether of capital that Crusoe seems "logical." Yet if you are a reader descended from the human beings traded into slavery, you would understand my position. Why are we carrying on with this protagonist if we are not seized by his ambition—and if we call it ambition in the beginning, now may we call it greed? Why do we proceed when the protagonist is so utterly foolish and venal?

Crusoe later speaks of the "load of guilt that bore down all his comfort,"[77] but this guilt seems strangely (for a reader like me) unconnected to his involvement with the slave trade and dehumanization for profit. Rather, it springs from his wilfulness against his father's wishes. It is an amoeba-like guilt, ubiquitous, ungrounded—or only grounded in some filial crime, some innate crime like that sin of Adam and Eve, so convenient and amorphous.

The English novels that come out of the Atlantic slave trade and its aftermath turn to the religious as a break and a salve—mirroring the religious arguments of the day that acted as a bolster for commerce and for regularizing populations moving through the industrial revolution. And these novels turn to illness to generate the religious, as well: the character is thrown into an otherworldliness by fevers that launch into spiritual reflection—but not reflection enough to cancel the allure of empire. Crusoe comes to good health to establish that he is "king and lord of all"—of this unknown place to which he is unattached except by shipwreck and noblesse oblige. All that piety, all that reckoning with God, all the religiosity that he experiences on the island is mere posturing, leading to another way in which white supremacy comes to think of itself as ordained by a god. None of these things are contradictory in the text—God and slavery are perfectly compatible; this is the way in which many novels of the period can dissertate on piety at the same time as their narratives are undergirded by slave owning, and earning wealth from misery and the immiseration of entire populations.

Why did Crusoe think this island was all his own? In the spirit of conquest in that age in the European cosmos: whatever one finds, even by accident, belongs to you. Crusoe may be a stranger on this island, but the fantasy is that it belongs to him. He thinks nothing of who might live there already, because the assumption is that no one does; and the conclusion, therefore, is that the island is his. But "no one" and "mine" are fabrications of the imperialist imagination. Crusoe's inventory of cocoa, orange, lemon, limes, grapes, etc. is the inventory of a business-man, not a survivor or a simple liver of life. This stock taking is mirrored in the gross and rapid economic expansion of the time, in the "discovery" and introduction of new "products" for middle-classing the European markets. Crusoe is taken up, inhabited, ideologized by this view of the world, which is inter-polated by, and part and parcel with, Christianity. Crusoe may speak of a load of guilt, but in a novel rife with inventory, the "load of guilt" goes un-itemized. There is a way in which the novels of the period turn uncomfortably to this religious soul-searching minus any clarity about the sins. This volta, the turn of thought, is of course the great enterprise of the taxonomy of colonialism, the age of carnage in Africa and the Americas.

Some contemporary readers might say, "Well, it was the time. Do not blame the author or his narrator for these ideas. The novel is a work of art. It cannot be reduced to this reading." But those readers cannot have it all ways. First, enslaved people also lived in their time—as narrators without an author. They lived in the same time as this novel's author and narrator, and any equivocation places and objectifies enslaved people as inanimate and inhuman, like a chair or an axe; it bestows once again the mantle of the human on the European. Yes, the text is a work of art—as we have come to define art. And yes, it is also reducible to its origins and its imaginaries, which are produced by its historical place, environment, quotidian details.

As we have seen, Crusoe's assertions of authority and claim to ownership of the island are givens for the reader. But how exactly does Crusoe own it? Even in his terms, whom has he paid for it? Of course, the idea is that such authority is a given, one that remains a constant within these lands that the Europeans claim to "acquire," having put patches of land under cultivation—or, having "discovered" growing things, and designating this as cultivation. Crusoe's description is that of a king or owner of everything; and despite the tongue-in-cheek undertone, it is nevertheless his real stance in describing the island. (What does Du Bois tell us? "Always, somehow, some way silently, but clearly, I am given to understand that whiteness is the ownership of the earth forever and ever, Amen!"[78]) Crusoe's psychological orientation—or let us say, his cultural orientation—is to assume a kind of God-given ownership of his surrounds.

Then, shortly after this aggrandizement and satisfaction, the ominous footprint appears in the sand. This footprint haunts all of English literature and beyond. In his novel *Crusoe's Footprint,* Patrick Chamoiseau would have us think it represents the philosophical call to acknowledge and confront the other, meaning the self, meaning the human—and he makes much of redeeming the narrator in his retelling, three hundred years later.

But a reader like me, in the moment of reading about this footprint, wishes for it to be a sign of Crusoe's demise. On the other hand, if the reader is hailed by the colonial aesthetic, of course she is as fearful as Crusoe. This footprint has generated so much narration, and this aesthetic has launched and animated so many novels, it leaves the original novel buried in novelistic practice and discourse to be perpetually exhumed and reanimated. This literary footprint has covered over so many real footprints that one cannot say the word "footprint" without having this footprint appear. This footprint is superseded only by the image of Christ's feet nailed to the cross. But the footprint is the image that worries the European novel—or the novel in general. It worries Albert Camus and it worries Cormac McCarthy. It is the European fear of, and disaffection with, other people.

There is a 1972 Werner Herzog film called *Aguirre, the Wrath of God*. It is perhaps the most honest European account of conquest I've experienced in a European work of the imagination. First, we see the steep mountain and clouds, then a red line of movement, then, closer still, a cannon and a priest, a statue of the Virgin Mary, two Spanish women awkwardly carried in covered litters, chained and enslaved Inca men being shoved and brutalized by conquistadors dressed in padded leather and beaten-iron clothing—all making their way down the Peruvian Andes. The conquistadors are looking for El Dorado with cannon and the Bible, this perfect couple, in the lead. And playing the sixteenth-century conquistador Lope de Aguirre is Klaus Kinski. His wreckage of a face is skeptical, plotting and sly, his body

moves like a skeleton, rickety and poised, the coordinated inco-
ordination of true violence; he is elegant. One cannon falls down
the mountain, one is fired randomly at everything and anything,
one raft spins and spins in a vortex on the Marañón River. All is
told with Kinski's body—Aguirre is clattering and slinky. You
spend the whole movie watching its stillness and its locomotion.
And the priest, Gaspar de Carvajal, on whose journal Werner
Herzog based the film, his face unbeatific and slightly grungy,
tells the desperate Inés, wife of Pedro de Ursúa, whom Aguirre
has had shot, "You know, my child, for the sake of our lord, the
Church has always been on the side of the strong." What truth.
When Ursúa is finally killed, Inés walks into the forest toward
whatever horrible fate she imagines, whatever horrible stories
have been told of the inhabitants, rather than stay with what she
has come to know as the true carnage. As they float by on the
river, Aguirre's puppet emperor of El Dorado, Don Fernando
de Guzmán, declares, "All the land we see to the left and all the
territory to the right now belongs to us. I solemnly and formally
take possession of all this land."

Conquest in the film is unadorned—no dreadful love stories,
no heraldic music, no chivalrous men—just the obsequious, the
craven, the greedy, the power-grabbing and the homicidal. It is
said that Francis Ford Coppola's *Apocalypse Now* was influenced
by Herzog's *Aguirre, the Wrath of God*. You can see that. But
Coppola's film is far too romantic, far too intent on American
moralism, mysticism and spectacle. Herzog's *Aguirre* is as
remorseless as conquest.

———

In *Robinson Crusoe* we read: "Yet I entertained such an abhorrence of the savage wretches that I have been speaking of, and of the wretched, inhuman custom of their devouring and eating one another up, that I continued pensive and sad, and kept close within my own circle for almost two years after this: when I say my own circle, I mean by it my three plantations—viz. my castle, my country seat (which I called my bower) and my enclosure in the woods."[79]

The white imagination is a wild thing, as witnessed here. Crusoe is terrified after seeing the footprint. He has never encountered so-called cannibals—he has only heard about them—but they feature in his fears, in his imaginings of peril and danger. And we take it for granted, that his fears are ours. Why do we not think, "Oh, finally he will be rescued"? Why do we not anticipate welcome and assistance from the Indigenous people? Because we have been prepared by all of the rehearsals of Euro-dominance in the text to expect "barbarians." What makes us ready, even in the twenty-first century, to expect barbarians? Even after all our readings, "*they*" remain the threat, not Crusoe.

Note, too, that what Crusoe calls his "circle" is his "three plantations." "As long as I kept my daily tour to the hill, to look out, so long also I kept up the vigour of my design, and my spirits seemed to be all the while in a suitable frame for so outrageous an execution as the killing twenty or thirty naked savages."[80] All of this is worked up in his imagination, to the point of him being prepared to commit mass murder despite not seeing a soul in his now-twenty years on the island.

Then the footprint appears. And then the Indigenous man.

He had a very good countenance, not a fierce and surly aspect, but seemed to have something very manly in his face; and yet he had all the sweetness and softness of a European in his countenance, too, especially when he smiled. His hair was long and black, not curled like wool; his forehead very high and large; and a great vivacity and sparkling sharpness in his eyes. The colour of his skin was not quite black, but very tawny; and yet not an ugly, yellow, nauseous tawny ... and first, I let him know his name should be Friday, which was the day I saved his life; I called him so for the memory of the time. I likewise taught him to say Master; and then let him know that was to be my name ...[81]

This is an amazing physical description: the Europeanizing of the figure, or the desire to describe the figure as being as close as possible to Euro notions of beauty, is intense, and acts as a kind of defamiliarizing of the figure Crusoe called the savage not long ago. Aphra Behn's Oroonoko is described in much the same terms—as being more European in features, so as to distinguish him from all characteristics attached to the African or the "native"; to mark difference as well as lack; to mediate slavery and to aggrandize the speaker's finer perceptions. "And yet he had all the sweetness and softness of a European in his countenance too." This is a bizarre attribution—the sweetness and softness of Europeans being oxymoronic throughout the age in which the novel is set, and beyond. The figure must also be distinguished from "the negroes"—even if this figure is later blackened or Africanized. It will be important, much later, to note the blackening of this figure in J.M. Coetzee's *Foe*. Though it is not the first instance of that transference.

Crusoe assumes this figure's obeisance, and organizes his subjection, accompanied by a healthy dose of religiosity and noblesse oblige. Defoe's dissertations on God and Providence stand in for philosophical thought, as do discourses on life and chance and choice, and ultimately on the superiority of European thinking. The Indigenous man is not afforded a consciousness, a sense of world or worlding; rather, he is assumed to be without these faculties. Given that these justifications which prove the superiority of Europeans exist right beside treatises on enslavement, they become, in effect, part of these treatises on enslavement. And in the logic of the novel, this all comes after the possession of the Indigenous man—meaning that this self-serving disquisition concludes with the idea that Providence smiles strangely but brightly on the narrator.

What follows in *Crusoe* is the education of the Indigenous man in Christianity, and also in agriculture. We are to believe, then, that Indigenous people did not eat or kill game—not animals nor birds nor fish, all which were plentiful—only people. The Taíno, the Arawak, the Carib, the Ciboney and the Warahoon lived thousands of years in these territories, but it is a European who teaches one of them how to hunt and fish and farm. This is, of course, utterly preposterous. (And one thinks of Oroonoko being taught by a European in the ways of princeliness or governance.) Meanwhile, Crusoe learns nothing from the Indigenous man's cosmology—or nothing except that which appears only for him to debunk. The chapter "Friday's Education" is crucial in this regard; it is here where the stakes in cosmology and hierarchy are laid out.

For example, in refuting, as he does here, the Indigenous myths of a deity, it appears that Crusoe must forget about Moses going to receive the tablets of commandments. The story of the Priests of the Indigenous peoples, Oowokakee, receiving the instructions of the god Benamuckee who "lived beyond all" is surely no stranger than that of Moses or any priest of the Christian Bible speaking to the Christian god. Yet all the cosmologies the European encounters, regardless of any similarity to his own, are dismissed in a reductive précis. Crusoe freely admits to recognizing a form of priesthood in the Indigenous man's account of his gods, but nevertheless goes on to impose his own cosmology as superior.

When faced, through the Indigenous man's inquiries, with the absurdity of Christianity, Crusoe cannot answer. Yet he places his doctrine higher than the doctrine of the Indigenous man. And something like receiving foolishness as gospel is required of that man, and of readers. What hypocrisy and forgetfulness. A reader like me is incredulous.

The philosophical tension in constant play in this novel is about what is human, and what is not; survival and sovereignty (Crusoe's, and the novel's, and European society's) depend on the answer. The author produces from the mouth of the Indigenous man the insistence that the European govern him, and insistence that *this* European become master of the Indigenous nations. A reader like me can only see the pedagogical work of empire in these exchanges. The book contains only sparse dialogue, in contrast to the abundant reportage, so these conversations matter. The general language of the book is riven through with imperialist intentions, and the assertion and persistence of this language is cumulatively tedious. Expressions such as *my island, my country, having dominion, I am king,* occur so often that they beat a note of urgency, a frenzied repetition.

As for the Indigenous people in the novel, they are represented as having a perpetual innocence—a representation that then moves from innocence to evil. The only purpose of this is to maintain the myth of Europeans as gods. The barbarity of the Europeans is elided while the so-called cannibalism of the Indigenous people is accentuated in service of this myth. Yet it is European barbarity that is in progress in the novel, just as it is in the historical period, on a massive scale. But, through elision, it does not stick to the bodies of the Spanish or the English; it sticks to the bodies of the Indigenous people.

Though they live together for several years, and though, Crusoe happily claims, the man has made his life worth living, he continues to refer to his fellow human as "savage." Nowhere in the following passage is the master/slave narrative disrupted, even as the paragraph calls for disruption, and even as the pages that follow equivocate over the presumption of moral superiority. We read:

> What authority or call [had I] to pretend to be judge and executioner upon these men as criminals.... How do I know what God Himself judges in this particular case? It is certain these people do not commit this as a crime; they think it no more a crime to kill a captive taken in

war than we do to kill an ox; or to eat human flesh than we do to eat mutton.

When I considered this a little, it followed necessarily that I was certainly in the wrong; that these people were not murderers, in the sense that I had before condemned them in my thoughts, any more than those Christians were murderers who often put to death the prisoners taken in battle; or more frequently, upon many occasions, put whole troops of men to the sword ... that this would justify the conduct of the Spaniards in all their barbarities practised in America, where they destroyed millions of these people; who, however they were idolators and barbarians, and had several bloody and barbarous rites in their customs, such as sacrificing human bodies to their idols, were yet, as to the Spaniards, very innocent people; and that the rooting them out of the country is spoken of with the utmost abhorrence and detestation by even the Spaniards themselves at this time, and by all other Christian nations of Europe, as a mere butchery, a bloody and unnatural piece of cruelty, unjustifiable either to God or man; and for which the very name of a Spaniard is reckoned to be frightful and terrible, to all people of humanity or of Christian compassion; as if the kingdom of Spain were particularly eminent for the produce of a race of men who were without principles of tenderness, or the common bowels of pity to the miserable, which is reckoned to be a mark of generous temper in the mind.[82]

Crusoe acknowledges that the Spaniards were brutal in wiping out the Indigenous people in some parts of the New World, and that those acts were no less brutal than cannibalism. This clarity, though, is partial. His own country of England is responsible for just as much carnage. The vaunted civilizing propaganda that reinforced the British Empire's colonial project is displayed in this critique of the Spaniards. Here, then, in the middle of the "adventure," is the English rivalry with the Spanish for the slave trade and conquest.

Crusoe makes some philosophical musings that approach a reconciliation with the idea that his existence and morality are not superior to those he calls savages. And despite all these equations, despite rethinking his life, rethinking God, rethinking Providence, rethinking what might be cultural difference and whether it might be wrong to judge peoples' customs, in the end what Crusoe mourns is that he did not stay in Brazil and become a rich planter, as he was on his way to becoming. What he mourns is that he sought to go to Africa to procure Black people for slavery instead of staying in Brazil and letting others do that for him, purchasing the Africans when they arrived in Brazil.

Even Crusoe's dreams are of savages and enslavement: before he encounters the Indigenous man, he dreams of him; and he imagines rescuing someone from these so-called savages, only to make the escapee his servant. And savages, of course, can only be servants or slaves. It seems that the prevailing European sensibility could not envision anyone encountered outside of it as human or equal or put on earth for anything but the purpose of servitude. Crusoe's very dreams, his imaginary games, contained the pleasure of how he would use this person, this savage, he encounters: "It came very warmly upon my thoughts, and indeed irresistibly, that now was the time to get me a servant, and, perhaps, a companion or assistant."[83]

Colonialism, then, was a set of arrangements designed and perceived to give pleasure. An aesthetic. A dream. A desire. And one no sooner dreamt than realized. The narrator procures his wish: a man, who, according to Crusoe, willingly becomes not his equal, or his friend, or even his fellow survivor, but "my savage." And as we have seen, like Aphra Behn's character of Oroonoko, this man, too—in order to bring him into a fold of recognizability, in order to make him legible to the white audience of the time and place him inside the scene of imperial domesticity—has all the "sweetness of a European countenance." By the time these two novels were written, the slavery economy was more than a hundred years old and only gaining in vigour. So much industry and daily life had been generated through it already, and "greater things" were still to come. The technologies of shipping, plantations-agriculture and manufacturing were in full blossom, and it would take between 120 and 200 years for chattel slavery to be brought to an end. Slavery, then, was not a minor feature of these years but their driving apparatus. And alongside monetary and political economies were the economies of representation of blackness and Indigeneity— fully developed not only in novels but in the production of painting, sculptures and other visual media, in newspapers and cartoons, and more.

———

How does the novel end? After twenty-eight years, Crusoe is rescued, and very appropriately he collects his money and his possessions and returns to the centre of colonialism. That is what we readers have been anticipating. The reader wants him to return to the regular life from which he has been plucked; the purpose of the whole adventure has been for him to return to this state—one in which he secures his own well-being through the slave trade and all its ambitions. We have not been fooled; we have eagerly participated in this endeavour. The underlying endeavour of the text is to have the protagonist saved from the possibility of never returning to his life—the life of the slave trader or the slave owner. Slavery is in full swing; and the Indigenous man accompanies Crusoe in various European travels, protecting Crusoe through various heroics.

The rest of the novel is about Crusoe's recovery of his capital and all the arrears of his thirty-five-year absence from England. It turns out that the whole book is about accounting: the lucrative endeavours of slavery, and the enormous wealth achieved. Today, economic textbooks employ Crusoe as an example of "Homo economicus" by abstracting hypothetical accounts of his economic behaviour. Matthew Watson draws this to our attention and critiques the contemporary use of this example in his essay, in *New Political Economy*, "Crusoe, Friday and the Raced Market Frame of Orthodox Economics Textbooks."[84] In such textbooks, Crusoe and Friday are laughably said to have a contract. And in them, Crusoe's desire is represented as not merely to find a way off the island, or even to find sustenance; instead, he is presented as a man who always makes economic action out of his life. No new understandings regarding freedom come to

Crusoe on this long exile. He is in exile, but *not* in a new world. Of course, racial hierarchies are economic hierarchies, as are gender hierarchies; and economics as a field is rife with, and buttressed by, suspension of disbelief. This is especially true of the colonial debts owed by the colonized, and the continued subordination of various economies to the former colonizer. In this bizarre reversal of worlds, expropriation becomes a debt owed by the one expropriated. And it is here, in this reversal, that we find "Friday."

Defoe's novel is breathless with accounting, always lodged in the language of honour and honesty and reward for Crusoe's travails: "It is impossible to express the flutterings of my very heart when I found all my wealth about me; for as the Brazil ships come all in fleets, the same ships which brought my letters brought my goods: and the effects were safe in the river before the letters came to my hand."[85]

The many rewritings of *Crusoe* over the years attest not only to the power of the narrative but to its symmetries with capital. They attest to the power of the aesthetic of capitalism as its own compelling genre. All one has to say is "desert island" to conjure *Crusoe*—and that trope is played out over and over in films, animation/cartoons, game shows, reality shows, board and video games, children's books. The economic model, and therefore the social model, for living is thereby reinscribed.

Marked throughout, in the language of the narrative, is this eternal subordination, this inability to see anyone except Europeans as human. This language implicates both Defoe's novel and Aphra Behn's—it is a blind spot, a deep contradiction in the pattern and narration of these stories, a petrifaction of philosophical ideas and a cementing of the terms of the human that will permeate all texts that use this pattern of telling and inquiry. A reader like me notices the continuing drag and pull of this novel; that one can read this adventure and its rewritings as a constant desire to reinforce these hierarchies. Each page is a justification for domination. That is the energy of the text—not the survival of the protagonist, but the survival of the hierarchy. *Crusoe* is such a tense book. We are led to believe that tension in such a book comes from the danger of the unknown, but in reality it comes from the desire for the viability of the colonial framework, the sponsorship of it, the sustenance of it and the survival of its creatures, its mores, its substance. The text is kinetic with this desire. And the adventure's end is the actualization, and triumph, of the colonial project. This is the tension/feeling that attends all "adventure." It is the "civilised" world, the world the protagonist carries in "his" body that is at risk in them. And he must return to that world in possession of the "other."

IV. when did "Friday" become Black and lose his tongue?

Ficre Ghebreyesus's painting returns to me here. There is no island in the painting *Solitary Boat in Red and Blue*. One doesn't get the sense of shipwreck or even shore in the conventional sense. The boat in the painting drifts toward perhaps a future more than a shore. It has become psychically untethered to those economies that set it adrift. And of course "we" are in the boat. A different "we" from the figure in Defoe's adventure. This boat is refuge from adventure. It is also refuge and escape from the closed meanings that adventure produces. However, written 267 years after *Robinson Crusoe*, and published in 1986, in the last decade of apartheid, J.M. Coetzee's *Foe* is drowned in its antecedent. It also gives us the colonially clarifying transference of the figure "Friday"—a transference from Indigenous to the Americas to African/Black. Susan Barton, the narrator of *Foe*, is Coetzee's intervention/invention into Defoe's imagination— or perhaps it is his continuation of that imaginary. *Foe* is steeped in something else—or we might say something greater—for its interlocution has accumulated weight through its many itera- tions and its many fascinations. To a reader like me, it is clear that its author is living in a world parallel to the world of Defoe.

When Susan Barton arrives shipwrecked on the same island as Crusoe, she is dressed in a petticoat. No sooner are we given this image than we are given another one: a white woman (in a petticoat) with a Black man hulking over her. When this figure "Friday" became Black or African in the imagination is anyone's guess, but somehow in *Foe* he is, and this makes perfect sense, of course, to any contemporary reader. In the schema of racial capital that this era navigates, radically oppositional subjects must be created; the elimination of nuance, particularly nuance about those who labour in its service, is necessary for racial capital's existence and continuation. The figure of the peoples who populated these Americas before European conquest, and are still on these lands—the Indigenous peoples—is no longer necessary to the story. The expropriation of their land is complete. And antagonisms are said to be laid to rest in that schema or considered not as urgent. But labour in racial capitalism, labour which came to be signified by blackness, is constant, necessary and ongoing—and so "Friday" has become who he is here, Black or African.

A reader like me gets it.

Let's look back at the moment when Defoe's narrator, stranded on the island, finds a body from another shipwreck: "He had no clothes on but a seaman's waistcoat, a pair of open-knee'd linen drawers, and a blue linen shirt; but nothing to direct me so much as to guess what nation he was of. He had nothing in his pockets but two pieces of eight and a tobacco pipe—the last was to me of ten times more value than the first."

How strange that it is a dead boy who arrives from the shipwreck—a boy wearing clothing strangely similar to that worn by the woman in *Foe*, according to Coetzee's description. Did Coetzee transform the desires animating the original description of the dead boy into the appearance of a woman on the island? More, did the desirous or tender tone of the original's language produce the figure/image of a woman to Coetzee? Or, to put it baldly, did the corpse of a drowned boy from another shipwreck occasion the invention of the woman in his novel *Foe*? Perhaps not, *Foe* is intervening in feminism's discourses of the '80s.

"All shipwrecks," Susan Barton remarks, do indeed "become the same shipwreck."[86] The repetition of story, the Euro-romance with blackness—*that* is the shipwreck from which the Black being must recover. A reader like me doesn't know how to begin to describe the horror story presented in *Foe*—a story that begins in all horrors. And here in *Foe* another invitation—one for a white woman to "play" in the dark. The demotic of racial capital is on full display here; the language markers are laid out. First, there is the appearance of the Black man and the description of his state, with his "white glint of teeth," "cracked feet" and "mimicry" of attempting to speak the thing the white man commands him to utter, and which he is unable to; there is the reference to his hair, like a strange material, and finally the dark stub of his tongue cut out by slavers. These macabre images and signs are then deployed relentlessly throughout the novel. Susan Barton asks, "Is Friday an imbecile?" "He has no tongue," Coetzee's Crusoe (or as the author names him, "Cruso") responds. And the question of "Friday's" sentience seems to be the rumination of the book—a rumination which finds no resolution. "If Providence were to watch over all of us," says Cruso, "who would be left to pick the cotton and cut the sugarcane? For the business of the world to prosper . . ."[87] Again I note that this book was written in the midst of sustained and ongoing resistance to apartheid in South Africa, and was published four or so years before the end of apartheid.

Why this further examination so many hundreds of years later when there is no revelation, only repetition—a repetition that feels like insistence? Who needs this figure of "Friday" anymore? Is it Freudian? Is it lazy allegory? Is it a mistake? If one were to set oneself the task of reimagining *The Life and Adventures of Robinson Crusoe*, and imagining a woman into it, then why not imagine more? Why produce this new but deadly-same interpretation?

Both in *Foe* and in the original, it never occurs to the protagonist or the novelist to imagine a world where "Friday" is not enslaved; it never occurs to them that those relations might be different. There is never the thought that relations between people on an island, even and especially an island populated by only two or three, might be re-apprehended. This failure owes its stiffness to the political economies of the times, which the authors produce reflexively, and the ideological soup both novels swim in. Instead, the same tropes are reiterated across the centuries and geographies that divide the authors, the same descriptions of the savage and child-like deployed. And the same theory of superiority observed, unbroken.

Tediously, because Susan Barton is a woman, the author must introduce a sexual encounter between her and Cruso. And tediously it must be a rape, which Barton must sublimate and/ or tolerate. This seems to be the reason for this woman to arrive in the novel, since we have little information about her own life or her motivations except the briefest outline of a lost daughter and a search for her. Other than that, it appears her *raison d'être* is to find the author Defoe, in order to continue the story of Cruso/e and, ironically, to transport the figure of Friday, now Black, through the text. The sexual encounter, which is to say the rape, and the protagonist's justification of it, recalls Lucy in Coetzee's later *Disgrace*. In that book, Lucy accounts for her rape as a kind of just tool by the men because they have suffered the violence of apartheid—as if women, white women in this case, must not only bear the violence of rape but must understand it as a male right, male expiation and national expiation. Meanwhile, in *Foe*, with the words "no doubt I might have freed myself," Susan Barton expresses the myth of women's complicity or culpability in their own rapes, and acquiescence to male violence.

"We yield to a stranger's embrace," says the protagonist, and were it not important to note the implications of this, one would laugh and reply, "Give me a frigging break."[88] The words are inexplicable. Why does yielding always fall to women to do? The same narrative soporific is at use here as in the subjugation of the Indigenous man in Defoe's original description: how that man "yields" to him, laying his head on Crusoe's leg in supplication. In *Foe*, the author must get the sexual encounter out of the way and settled to establish a bond between Cruso and Susan, albeit one that is violent. Now Susan's whole attention is focused on Cruso, on describing him and not herself. We never know about her despair or the terrible conditions that led to her finding herself shipwrecked and flung up on the island in a petticoat. A reader like me asks, Why this avatar? If the author's intention is to write this novel from the point of view of a woman, the novel hardly accomplishes that, since Barton's purpose is not to tell her own story but to reprise Cruso's. Her own life appears ghostly, and the search for her daughter, her purposes for traveling, remain tangential to the fiction. Even when her daughter appears later in the novel, in a ghost-like dream, it bears no relation to this story—and the arrival is too late for it to have any value. It seems an afterthought of the author.

Rather, the two main theses of the novel, which are tattooed out over the course of the next hundred pages, revolve around these questions: "What had held Friday back all these years from beating in his master's head with a stone while he slept, so bringing slavehood to an end and inaugurating a reign of idleness? And what held Cruso back from tying Friday to a post every night, like a dog, to sleep the more secure, or from blinding him, as they blind asses in Brazil?"[89] Each question is a confirmation of its underlying affirmations. And each, in this instantiation of the adventures hundreds of years later, contains an historical falsehood: in fact, every slave owner feared and expected revolt (recall Aphra Behn); and every slave owner committed acts of barbarity toward the enslaved, beginning with the original act of enslavement. Each question is also a narrative disavowal by the author, put into the mouth of Susan Barton. Here we have the disavowal of slave narratives, legal histories and cases, the *Code noir*—all to reprise the same logics that animated the original narrative. Who wonders about these propositions, now or then? It is an odd conceit to always proceed from this particular kind of wonder. Why not instead imagine that two or three people, finding themselves on an island away from the regimes of the slavocracy, might imagine sovereignty? Why not imagine that they might want to enter a different set of relations?

What a wild, unthought thought.

Throughout *Foe*, the narrator's minstrel descriptions of the Friday figure are something to behold. With his tuneless tune, his silent silence, he is a representation of representation, nothing else. White critics see, and want to see, significance in this characterization, but it is nothing except banal. Of all the things the novelist could imagine, of all the possible turnarounds, we land in sameness. Defoe's take is understandable—there's no pretense in it; Coetzee's take, not so much. I write this not to imagine "Friday," or to call for any reimagining of this avatar (I will never carry on the endeavour of rewriting these tales), but to cast a glimmer of light on the existed/existing but as yet unimagined world. In contrast, the contemporary imagination, inside and outside of literature, seems to be wound up with the necrotic world of Crusoe. The world of the book, and the world of the world that the book gestures to, have a deadening symmetry to which Coetzee is bound. One cannot court the contemporaneous and retreat from its demands. One cannot both rewrite an imagined world and shirk from it at the same time.

In *Foe*, Susan Barton and Cruso are finally rescued and Friday runs away, whereupon Barton urges the ship's captain to capture him, since he is a "slave and a child."[90] She does not see Friday's escape *as* escape; instead, she assigns a perpetual childishness to him and by extension to all Black people. Friday could not possibly be escaping. His freedom from continued slavery cannot possibly have occurred to him at the sight of the ship.

And then Susan Barton has sex with a dying, unresponsive Cruso on board the rescue ship, in an act of what can only be described as authorial misogyny. Coetzee's narrator is a kind of cipher or container of all the sexist tropes of the contemporary. Unlike the protagonist in *The Wall* by Marlen Haushofer, who is stranded behind an invisible wall, after an unknown catastrophe has seemingly overtaken the world. Having to fend for herself, she is the antithesis of Crusoe and of *Foe*'s Susan Barton. Unlike Barton she experiences transformation, and a self-awareness beyond, and escaping, rehabilitations of masculinities. She writes, "My body, more skillful than myself, had adapted itself and limited the burdens of my femininity to a minimum."[91] In response to the prurient violence of such narratives of "adventure" she writes, "I find it striking that I've never noted in my diary when I shot a deer. I now recall that the idea of writing it down simply repelled me; it was quite enough that I had to do it."[92]

Of course, I see that it is compelling for some—if not for me—to rewrite this adventure. It is compelling, if this is the narrative that haunts all narrative, and this the structure that haunts all structure. Yet in the case of *Foe*, the retelling functions to reimbue and repeat all the dreadful notions of the dread. In general are these retellings similar to that of a child who writes a page from a lesson over and over, repeating it to get the pattern of sentences? "And what are these patterns?" a reader like me, then asks. To this reader, the rewriting is a deadly and boring exercise of reinscribing a vision of Black people as figures upon which lessons of sentence, lessons of grammar, lessons of restriction must be administered.

In *Foe*, also telling is Susan Barton's thesis on benevolence and violence. When she "teaches" Friday something through benevolence, his lack of understanding brings her to violence, and she confesses to understanding why "a man will choose to be a slave owner." Benevolence here then is a subset of violence. "'All my efforts to bring Friday to speech, or to bring speech to Friday, have failed,' I said. 'He utters himself only in music and dancing, which are to speech as cries and shouts are to words. There are times when I ask myself whether in his earlier life he had the slightest mastery of language, whether he knows what kind of thing language is.'"[93]

A reader like me is, by this time, nauseous from this play; this play with and around the figure of Friday is remarkable only in what it reveals about the place and use of blackness in the white imagination. It is a lake and eye, a sea. A silence, something at the heart of the story. Despite gestures or vanities or attempts at discourse about who speaks for whom, or who is capable of expression, or if it is possible to write in the voices of others, *Foe* fails to wrestle with the material conditions of the making of literature, the making of the characters, the making of the author.

Mimicking Defoe's summaries on God and Providence, Coetzee comes up with his own set of obfuscations:

We, or some of us: it is possible that some of us are not written, but merely are; or else (I think principally of Friday) are written by another and darker author. Nevertheless, God's writing stands as an instance of a writing without speech. Speech is but a means through which the word may be uttered, it is not the word itself.[94]

Coetzee's segue into the "philosophical" is not an improvement, insofar as it remains one of justification for the failure of self-reflection. Furthermore, the Black is that which is written upon; it remains the written-upon; it is the cipher for the legibility of white discourse, the rehearsal for its grander feelings, its imperialist views.

The hulking, sleeping presence of Friday is always, in *Foe*, close to the ongoing life of the other protagonists, watching, waiting to be told or instructed or discoursed about.

> Should I liberate him into a world of wolves and expect to be commended for it? What liberation is it to be packed off to Jamaica, or turned out of doors into the night with a shilling in your hand? Even in his native Africa, dumb and friendless, would he know freedom? There is an urging that we feel, all of us, in our hearts, to be free; yet which of us can say what freedom truly is? When I am rid of Friday, will I then know freedom? Was Cruso free, that was despot of an island all his own? If so, it brought no joy to him that I could discover. As to Friday, how can Friday know what freedom means when he barely knows his name?[95]

The novel asks, "Can Black people be trusted with freedom?" And: "If we free them, will they know how to handle it?" No peroration can refuse this meaning in *Foe*. The sentence "Should I liberate him into a world of wolves?" refuses the free will that is so vaunted in Euro-capitalist fantasies of "humanity." The pseudo-conversation about "Friday's sentience" has pervaded the white imagination. It is the elision that has taken hold of that white imagination, giving cover to the factual mathematics of wealth and extraction. And even when pointing out the unavailability of blackness to that white imagination, that lack in the white imagination is transmuted into a characteristic of blackness, a "lack" in the Black.

James Weldon Johnson's *The Autobiography of an Ex-colored Man*, first published in 1912, puts it this way: "And this is the dwarfing, warping, distorting influence which operates upon each and every colored man in the United States. He is forced to take his outlook on all things, not from the viewpoint of a citizen, or a man, or even a human being, but from the viewpoint of a colored man. It is wonderful to me that the race has progressed so broadly as it has, since most of its thought and all of its activity must run through the narrow neck of this one funnel."[96]

One wonders whether *Foe* would be a different novel if such a piece of insight about that "distorting influence," or this key work of James Weldon Johnson, had been available to the author. Perhaps Friday would not appear tongueless, lying in his corner, uncommunicative. Johnson's novel pre-empts the ruminations in Foe, and if one considers this knowledge, one arrives at the discourse in a different place. James Weldon Johnson elaborates:

And it is this, too, which makes the colored people of this country, in reality, a mystery to the whites. It is a difficult thing for a white man to learn what a colored man really thinks; because, generally, with the latter an additional and different light must be brought to bear on what he thinks; and his thoughts are often influenced by considerations so delicate and subtle that it would be impossible for him to confess or explain them to one of the opposite race. This gives to every colored man, in proportion to his intellectuality, a sort of dual personality; there is one phase of him which is disclosed only in the freemasonry of his own race.[97]

What if Coetzee had considered Babo, the character in Herman Melville's perceptive 1855 novella *Benito Cereno*, in his re-writing of Defoe's Friday? Melville's Babo, along with other Black people captured and being transported into slavery in the New World, seize a Spanish slave ship and its captain, Benito Cereno. Babo, the leader of the revolt, becomes the true captain of the ship, and he forces Cereno and the white sailors aboard to pretend to be in charge of the ship as the Black people try to find their way back to Africa. The ship soon becomes stuck in the doldrums, where it is discovered by another ship's captain, Delano. What appears to Captain Delano to be Babo's faithfulness to Benito Cereno turns out to be Babo holding Cereno and the white crew hostage. And what seems to be the order of things on board the vessel turns out to be quite the opposite. Delano leaves the ship thinking all is well until, in desperation, Cereno leaps off the vessel into a rowboat. Babo follows, with a knife to Cereno's throat. Only then does Delano realize the truth—and understands that Babo had intended to capture Delano's ship also. Cereno's ship is recaptured, the revolt violently put down, and Babo, refusing to say a word in his defense, is put to death. "Some months after, dragged to the gibbet at the tail of a mule, the black met his voiceless end. The body was burned to ashes; but for many days, the head, that hive of subtlety, fixed on a pole in the Plaza, met, unabashed, the gaze of the whites."[98]

Cereno is profoundly affected by the experience. The exchange that follows between Delano and Cereno occurs after the vessel is recaptured and on its way to Lima, and it speaks to Cereno's reconfigured world view.

> Again and again it was repeated, how hard it had been to enact the part forced on the Spaniard by Babo....
>
> "You are saved, Don Benito," cried Captain Delano, more and more astonished and pained; "you are saved; what has cast such a shadow upon you?"
>
> "The Negro."
>
> There was silence, while the moody man sat, slowly and unconsciously gathering his mantle about him, as if it were a pall. There was no more conversation that day.[99]

The passage questions the characterization of blackness that others imagine they know, or the transparency they have been deluded into believing, which is a corollary to the trade in slaves. Cereno is struck silent by Babo's—and that of the other captive Africans—desire and intention to be free. This silence is broken when he utters "the Negro"—a phrase filled with awe and disbelief, marking a profound psychic break. The characterizations of blackness that Cereno (and Delano) have been deluded into believing have been shattered.

To write like the master in the master narrative—that is one of the compulsions writers have. To rewrite the master narrative.

To join the "what if." What if a (white) woman appeared on the island? But this is all too simple a question to ask now, in the face of so much history, in the face of so much that is present. What is the point of rewriting the master narrative, one might ask, in light of all that we know? In the case of *Foe,* it is not a rewriting, even if a white woman appears. It is only a re-copying. A trace.

Character is about making a subject, and as a tool of literary production it is infused with practices that take as their premise an unavailable, and hence non-existent, Black sentience. This premise is, I think, embedded in the very idea of a protagonist: the dominant literary intelligence (following on a set of now-intuitive social practices that are reflected in literary form) posits white sociality as the default for, and *a priori* essential to, the "protagonist."

Ignoring the centrality of the Black subject to the white subject/imagination is a "convenient abstraction," to paraphrase Eduardo Galeano in *In Defence of the Word*, where he wrote of the necessity to be specific in literary address. Character is not neutral or empty; it is a live and active mode, transporting sedimented ideas. And as such, it is constantly outlining/defining/locating and embedding the presence of Black people in literary texts—the surprise of it; their sphinx-like appearance signifying everything and nothing. As Chinua Achebe said, "stories are not innocent."[100] And so, when I read *Foe* I see there all the thick, curdling histories it disavows, all the sedimented mathematics it ignores, all the sophistry it rehearses and all the discredited theories it proposes anew.

V. why save that?

In *Crusoe's Footprint*, or *L'empreinte à Crusoé*, by Patrick Chamoiseau (published in French in 2012; translated into English in 2022), the author writes this passage in the voice of "Crusoe":

> The mystery of my origin had tortured me for quite some time, but the torment of my survival quickly took the upper hand; . . . in this gap that served as my memory, something was still troubling me . . . it was not the details surrounding my origin, nor its very truth; I felt that it was linked to something unbearable, an immense pain . . . within me, indecipherably inscribed; I bore the suffering without knowing what it could be, especially since I kept trying to convince myself that the origin didn't matter.[101]

Chamoiseau's Crusoe, unlike other literary recountings, is unsure of his "identity" or his origin. He only comes by the name Crusoe when he reads the stitching on a strap that he finds wrapped around his body when propelled ashore from a wreckage. He holds on to the evidence from the wreckage, and his imagination tellingly provides the rest. But the gaze of this Crusoe is from another cosmology—a cosmology intercepted by colonialism, or inhibited from its own future. In its main disquisition, *Crusoe's Footprint* takes its protagonist on a philosophical search for being—and importantly, being "*in relation*." The crucial thesis of the book is that Chamoiseau's Crusoe must observe the world in relation.

I started to inhabit my name, Robinson Crusoe, to dig a place for myself; the objects brought back from the frigate nourished my imagination with a Western perspective . . . many a strange thing seemingly from my inner self added to this— . . . a jackal's arrival that troubles the gods . . . black and white lizards that weave cloths . . . twins in a millet calabash . . . bracelets of priests clinking against the sides of a horned mask . . . —but they were so incompatible with the rest of my evocations that I attributed them to residual memories belonging to some boastful sailor I had allegedly met; in fact, reconstructing my imagination from these objects bound to my obscure memory led only to chaos: any possibility of demystifying my origins would then disappear.[102]

Here we read doubleness and delirium, the apprehension of connection and disconnection; here we can discern pre-capitalist origins, the sensorium of colonialism shadowed by and overwritten by the possible selves emerging and vanishing, but still beckoning toward a different future. Here Chamoiseau presents the pretext for colonization, and the invention of colonial narrative as a story worked into legend, then written and rewritten so as to make anything else unrecognizable. This author's Crusoe is a much more complex figure because of this doubleness, as we are not certain where he emerges from, or who he really is— even though we have the outline of Defoe's Crusoe always in attendance. But Chamoiseau's conjuring of doubleness allows the author to work with the synergies of colonial thought even as that very system imposes recognition and assimilation: "I now knew that one is shaped also by his 'expression,' with which one stands; . . . . but 'expression' is not meant to be understood (just like all literature I suppose)—its initial use is to construct the authority of the one who activates it."[103]

This Crusoe, in his doubleness, lays out the legitimizing apparatus of colonial laws in their dense arbitrariness. As he describes colonial ideology, he points to its absurdities, its grandiosities, its macabre and fanciful imagination. While mirroring the original novel, in the scene where Crusoe lays out his dominion, Chamoiseau mocks this regimen and its elaborate apparatus:

> . . . I told myself occasionally that over the millennia the scepter of civilization was transmitted from chosen people to chosen people, . . . now it had fallen upon me—
>
> . . . I stood tall on one of those headlands, the ocean crashing below . . . and I kept it at bay by way of a great deal of proclamations, decrees, letters patent, and advanced police measures . . . article 7 of my Maritime Code forbade all waves to display as black or dark, . . . I put storms in order, . . . I dealt with boxfish catching, barring entry to venomous fish, crab distribution, turtle invasions, shipwreck possession, or treasures that the waves were authorized to deposit without taxation.[104]

Chamoiseau itemizes the accumulation of laws of dominance in a foolish array that illustrates the absurdity of these laws as well as the effects of their impositions. This rings true to our current world where, for example, maritime laws privatize the oceans and climate predictions go unheeded.

My official huts one after the other, Police Station,
Customs, Department of Weights and Measures, Office
of Land Registry, Office of Coastlines and Borders,
Heritage Museum, Department of Defense, Institute of
Natural Sciences, School of Cartography . . . were more
often empty than not, with a stool, a writing desk, a
candle, a duck quill, a calabash bowl filled with fish
ink, a relic of registry. . . . Normally, I sat in each office,
taking turns, according to a seasonal procedure largely
unchanged, and I thought about State affairs, made decisions, proclaimed decrees and orders. . . . I also inspected
my stock, my secondary caves, my emergency fortifica-
tions, my ramparts and watchtowers.[105]

Chamoiseau proceeds to outline and mirror Crusoe's original
colonization of the island, but now as a model of the European colonial apparatus—and of the models of governing that
those colonial powers took everywhere in the world. Here we
have the order of empire, imagined. It is an order that Crusoe
needs to exist; and outside of its order exists only what is
deemed savagery and terror. In Chamoiseau's hands, it is almost
a picture of hilarity—were it not true.

About Crusoe's discovery of the footprint and the alarm that
fills him as a result, Chamoiseau suggests that one fears "the
other as one desires the other"—as one fears and simultaneously
desires one's opposite or apposite. In Chamoiseau's novel, Crusoe
goes in search of the other, the other that he fears—but here the
discourse is slightly ahistorical or suggests an essential being
moving toward itself.

What Chamoiseau gets at is this: that the footprint haunting literature is a spectre of the colonized, a threat both in real and imagined terms; a spectre hanging over the whole enterprise of colonization and slavery.

On the one hand, Crusoe's relation to the absence speaks of, and is filled with, Euro-fantasies of blackness and Indigeneity. The sighting of the footprint raises a catalogue of racist typology, drawn from many continents and lands: "I saw him among his people in the midst of dark and mysterious ceremonies where he drank juices from stones and read prophecies spread across the stars; I saw him worship feathers and claim to be from a saurian family next to imperturbable rivers . . . ; he must have carried away the intestines of his relatives in the large shell of a funeral urn, which allowed him to talk to whatever evil was in the sky; he must have grilled red corn when his wives gave birth or ordered it to rain handfuls of pollen."[106]

The punctuating "I saw . . ." here is the insistent tattoo of codification—the codification of a "brutal imagination," to use the expression of the poet Cornelius Eady.

At the same time, the sighting of the footprint causes a crisis of existence in Chamoiseau's Crusoe, a crisis that makes him consider what it is to be human. In Chamoiseau's text, *terra nullius*, or an Edenic world, existed before colonialism; yet the text as a whole cannot help but be about the rehabilitation of the European in light of colonialism. Its address cannot be anything but a lesson to Europeans—a talking back to, but not talking beyond, European feeling. There is a sidelong gaze here; in other words, the "self" referred to in Chamoiseau's text cannot be the self of the enslaved or the colonized. The point of view is always skewed to the European, its particular dilemmas and concepts. The parable is the parable of Euro-consciousness. Despite what we come to know of Chamoiseau's Crusoe, most explosively his origin, in the end this too is tied to Euro-empire; put to the service of European rehabilitation. Even the author's surprising turn which, might have been more stunningly turned to another "we" remains an empty shell to be filled with ideas of awakening European humanity.

This Crusoe figure experiences a breakage with the man produced by empire and returns to a state of nature, a state of open perception. But we must ask: Why this return to a "state of nature" to procure redemption for this character? It seems to me that this Crusoe character is appointed for redemption in order to reinvigorate a philosophy of humanism that we know is riven through with states of slavery. It is a well-known genre, a well-known anticolonial strategy—yet one that keeps white humanity at the centre, one in which the other exists as a backdrop to white life, or for the education of white life. Why does Chamoiseau need this particular figure of Crusoe in order to look again? It is not as if looking again at Crusoe will redeem this character. But more important, why rehabilitate this figure at all? Why is this figure held up as the one through which all of us must think about the ideas and urgencies of the times—the self, the human, the just?

Chamoiseau posits Crusoe as a figure who experiences a kind of splitting of the self, or recognition of the self as both I and other. He discovers his own fear, his own footprint. And if the footprint is Crusoe's own, the tale of Robinson Crusoe is one of recognitions as well as fantasies—and fantasy it no doubt is, in its estimation of the Indigenous peoples of the Americas as well as the peoples of the continent of Africa. This transition, this almost-euphoric break, in the novel allows Chamoiseau's Crusoe to understand himself as living in the relation that Glissant proposes, rather than living in domination. He lives in heterogeneity, as Wilson Harris proposes. We read, "I was free because I was freed from all of that; I no longer desired to own or eat everything; I no longer feared starvation or shortage."[107]

Crusoe's diary or account is no longer a fiduciary account of experiences of economy, but a revelation of living in relation. It no longer expresses the prose of capitalism but the poetry of relation. As part of this process, Crusoe devalues all he had valued, returning the island to its original state, tearing down his fences and pipes for irrigation, ridding the island of his imposed economies of colonialism. The footprint remains a haunting throughout most of the work: indestructible, ubiquitous. When Crusoe isn't looking at it, he is thinking about it. The inference is that it is impossible to eradicate all traces of the other.

Still, I cannot fathom why we must visit these ideas through this character. Of course, the author understands the great hold that this text has on the literary imagination, and his refashioning draws attention to its flaws, but his faith in the possibilities of such a character's redemption, his faith that the transformation of the figure is of interest or possible, is more than a reader like me would give. A figure such as Crusoe is not, for this reader, worthy of reclamation. Moreover, the narrative's eventual turn toward the classics and the poetry of Parmenides is not fruitful. A return to "the ancients" does not mitigate the harms of colonialism—the classics informed colonialism and chattel slavery. And Chamoiseau's overarching thesis of Crusoe being "in relation" elides the ever-present gestures of control and conquest, and is a kind of overweening fantasy. How does one live in relation when one faces conquest and annihilation? What is the fate of "Friday" in this? The footprint appears as existential and unattached to a set of relations; it is abstracted from its relation.

At the end comes a surprise that a reader is little prepared for (although there are indications of it throughout): the Crusoe we encounter in this work is a delusional Dogon man who thinks himself to be Crusoe after he is shipwrecked and finds the name attached to him. This is revelatory in a number of ways. To discover that we have been inhabited by coloniality is not uncommon. To discover that, according to the captain, this man is not "Crusoe the Englishman" but Crusoe, a Dogon man, makes marvellous sense to many of us: we know how to inhabit whiteness—we who know the desires of, and the trophies for, inhabiting whiteness—learning the languages, the talk, the philosophies of whiteness; we are porous with whiteness and it begins here, in this period of conquest and pacification of the world into these regimes of coloniality. This period in which the novel is set is when all other knowledges are subsumed, are coerced, are overpowered by the colonial projects of every European power. This is when the chartered companies for supply, management, expropriation and exploitation began: the Royal African Company, the Dutch West India Company, the Danish West India Company, the French East India Company, the Compagnie des îles de l'Amérique, El Real y Supremo Consejo de las Indias, from Lançarote de Lagos to the papal bulls of

Nicholas V, to the Captaincies of the Colonies (Portuguese). This is when the British Empire gets its name.

It is laughable to read, in our contemporary moment, that studies and research must be conducted to, for example, find out about whether the British Crown or the Papal State benefited from slavery, or whether any European nation benefited from slavery and plantation economies, let alone universities and what might be now considered old money. Old money was then new money, in the period of slavocracy and conquest. (Anna Julia Cooper writes, in *A Voice From The South*, "Then, too, the South represented blood—not red blood, but blue blood. The difference is in the length of the stream and your distance from its source. If your own father was a pirate, a, robber, a murderer, his hands are dyed in red blood, and you don't say very much about it. But if your great great great grandfather's grandfather stole and pillaged and slew, and you can prove it, your blood has become blue and you are at great pains to establish the relationship."[108]) As Toni Morrison's character Baby Suggs says in *Beloved* when Sethe suggests that they might move to another house: "What'd be the point? . . . Not a house in the country ain't packed to the rafters with some dead Negro's grief."[109] You want to say of these disingenuous research projects, "What'd be the point? . . . Not a nation in this world. . . ." Or, to quote Morrison again, "The overweening, defining event of the modern world is the mass movement of raced populations, beginning with the largest forced transfer of people in the history of the world: slavery. The consequences of which transfer have determined all the wars following it as well as the current ones being waged on every continent."[110]

In his notes at the end of his book, Chamoiseau remarks: "It's sad: Defoe's Crusoe was a slave trader."[111] But this reader asks, why is that sad? It is sad only if you want to read the tale as universal, or if you wish to read the human as universal rather than an invention of post-slavery Europe. It is sad if you wish to read Defoe or Crusoe as the universal man. I am not sad that Crusoe was a slaver. I am sad that I have had to read him as the universal human. I have no hopes for any aspect of him that I might, for want of his being a slave trader, favour. I would echo the words writer Rinaldo Walcott said to me in a conversation: that "Friday becomes a 'thing' upon European contact, and he is drafted into the humanist project as both barbarous and passive, worth rescuing but not freeing."

The island where Crusoe is shipwrecked is surely in a time warp, as Chamoiseau remarks in his afternotes, and the effects of Defoe's narrative extend through time. "What matters," Chamoiseau writes, is "the existential situation in relation to our contemporary challenges."

And yes, *The Life and Adventures of Robinson Crusoe* is a palimpsest powerful enough to dislodge the word "footprint" from other meanings in my own mind, but the adventures it depicts are not beautiful. (Before these *Adventures*, the footprint was a lovely game of my childhood. On the beach at Guaya, it was a game with what we called the sea, which was the Atlantic Ocean. This game involved having our footsteps washed away. We would run toward the receding tide, put our footprints on the sand and run away as the tide came to claim them again.) But there is no particular significance, much less is there any beauty, in rewriting these eighteenth- and nineteenth-century novels;

there is nothing more that they may yield except to deepen the thrall in which they hold us, the thrall of the colonial world.

These rewritings put me in mind of contemporary visual artists who recreate the art of those periods, replacing white bodies with Black bodies—such as Kehinde Wiley, who painted *Rumors of War*. In my view such portraits create no disruption in the narratives of the paintings, except for some initial and brief surprise. Another register in which to read these works might be that of parody, and perhaps this is the deepest, most generous interpretation to make. It might even be sufficient. But the corpus of triumphalist white heroic painting overwhelms and seduces the renewed portraits—and reverberates in European painting itself not as parody but as envy and admiration; as desire.

I had thought, when I began to write these words, that I might relate Chamoiseau to Wilson Harris. But I find now that I was mistaken. *Palace of the Peacock*, by Wilson Harris, is a narrative that requires no callus to withstand or elide the violence of one's absent presence. For me, it is an origin novel in its subject as well as its method. It practices what Édouard Glissant calls "opacity." The event is the event of the colonial, but all elements, all characters, are present and in flux.

In *Palace of the Peacock,* the "I" narrator—who is singular, dual and multiple—writes:

> . . . I searched for words with a sudden terrible rage at
> the difficulty I experienced . . . "it's an inapprehension
> of substance," I blurted out, "an actual fear . . . fear of

life . . . fear of the substance of life, fear of the substance
of the folk, a cannibal blind fear in oneself. Put it how
you like," I cried, "it's fear of acknowledging the true
substance of life. . . . And somebody," I declared, "must
demonstrate the unity of being, and *show* . . ." I had
grown violent and emphatic . . . "that fear is nothing
but a dream and an appearance . . . even death . . ." I
stopped abruptly.[112]

The tale is of a journey into the forests of Guyana with all the
pre- and post-Columbian actors. Within the structure of the
novel, you are never fully aware of the journey's purpose or assured
of its outcome. It is a reckoning with coloniality. And since
coloniality seeks to order its human objects in particular ways,
including through narration and narrative style, Harris's novel
refuses that narration, and narrative style. Rather he chooses a
more complex narration, one that truly is simultaneous, and resistant to identification with the protagonist. He uses a multifocal
lens, with multiple and shifting points of view—as if attempting to make the reader see and hear everyone at once, and to
read everything at once. Kenneth Ramchand points out that
Harris disliked "the novel of persuasion" and felt that "since the
'medium' had been conditioned by previous use and framed by
ruling ideologies, there has to be an assault upon the medium
including not only the form of the novel but also the premises
about language that are inscribed in the novel."[113]

In *Caribbean Discourse,* Édouard Glissant writes about the
importance of form when thinking about the ghosts of colonialism, ghosts that reverberate in the present and into the future. For

him, narrative "implode[s] in us in clumps" and we are "transported to fields of oblivions, where we must, with difficulty and pain, put it all back together."[114] In *Palace of The Peacock,* Harris manages to fracture that European figure, and to place it in a relation where its own recovery was at stake or implicated or imperilled but our stake in the figure is not required. Harris points to other origins for his narrative and stays with them. His project, it seems to me, is to make a new human out of the wreck of Enlightenment discourse and its production of negation.

The problem for me, then, in *Crusoe's Footprint* (and as anticipated in Chamoiseau's own afternotes), is whether any recreation can be a variation. My thinking is that any attempted variation may be a reimposition, in the case of these texts. The variations continue to make the original texts the origin of everything.

These seventeenth-, eighteenth-, and nineteenth-century narratives were never naive, as Chamoiseau so forgivingly calls them. These fictions were compelling precisely because they spoke of their times, and were invested in their times, and also invested in the future their time predicted—no, authorized. And they were popular as a genre precisely because they did so.

Crusoe, of course, doesn't make himself over; he makes the slave trader the Man of the Century. He returns to England and to the wealth he has accumulated and to his life—to even more of his life.

We may read the denouement we discover in *Crusoe's Footprint*—that Crusoe is in fact the deranged Dogon man—as the derangement of coloniality and its effects, material and psychological, on the consciousness of Black people. These are the effects of a regime sometimes so thorough in its subjugation as to create, in the minds/consciousness of the oppressed, the simulacra of itself. The fact that Chamoiseau reveals "Crusoe" to be Dogon ties the trade to the continent's elites and ruling forces, and to their collusion in it. But this happens at a superficial level. On another level, Chamoiseau points to the dominant consciousness of the period, and this dominant consciousness is white supremacy. That the Dogon sailor remembers himself as white, as Crusoe, in his altered consciousness, or may be considered as "mad," speaks to Fanon's *Black Skin, White Masks* or to DuBois's double consciousness. It locates the imaginary as a white one, hostile to any other.

Rehabilitating the white consciousness that perpetuated slavery is one way that blackness is situated in the white imagination. Black writers have been given the project of this rehabilitation for centuries. White consciousness has occupied millions of sentences—with Black character situating itself around that consciousness in supplicant ways, coaxing it, tending to it, trying not to offend it, flattering it, or challenging it with the right degree of deference and, in myriad ways, cultivating it. To me white consciousness does not need rehabilitation; what needs centering is the Dogon consciousness hidden, overtaken, occluded in Chamoiseau's Crusoe. This is a consciousness Chamoiseau gestures strongly to, but which ultimately becomes a shadow set against European enlightenment and its abstruse racism.

Has white consciousness and its colonial projects so overwhelmed the present? Why does it need attending to rather than eliminating? Why must we be tied to its rehabilitation and its evolution (as in Chamoiseau's narrator's transcriptions of a Greek text)? I have always found this "clasp," this implied "duty," suffocating, and these narrations binding, veiling, stifling. And ultimately, useless. Since, so much of literary production has already been expended on this duty without improvement.

VI. these paragraphs are about a body

Perhaps the proposition that Friday (now the owner of two or more bodies—Black and Garifuna/Carib/Arawak) is resistant to interpretation might fascinate some, but it doesn't fascinate this reader. Even the proposition that Friday is Crusoe and Crusoe is Friday—mirrors, doppelgängers, the other—even this is unbearably, unnecessarily contorted for this reader. Friday sits in all texts as the always signed, the indelible, as well as, perversely, the illegible, and no play with this trope breaks or refashions it, because it is a sign. It is a liberal interpretation of the world, one that in keeping the trope alive exposes reflexively liberalism's "own" resistance to understanding. It points to liberalism's own rehabilitation—a rehabilitation lodged in its Christian core. Friday is the constitutive outside, against which the subject forms itself. The Friday figure has nothing to do with anything some of us know except that the figure appears as interruption, and as exhaustion with an uninteresting query that is also violent. It is a query that one is invited to take as benign, even as it is, in fact, deeply threatening. Friday's silence is silence—and always is, and always will be, silence in the cosmology of the liberal interpreter. The figure presented as figure is always figure. It is impossible to plop Friday down into any text and anticipate transformation of any kind. Friday's function is to be an unchanging sign, a fixed point in liberalism's equation. Any re-narrations sit in the viscosity of the original narrative/interpretation.

But there is another archive we might explore, an archive of the intellectual life and human activity that somewhat contemporaneously addressed questions of humanism and silence. For the last three hundred or so years, other narratives have been available to the imagination—in non-fiction like *The Letters of the Late Ignatius Sancho* (written between 1768 and 1780) or Quobna Ottobah Cugoana's *Thoughts and Sentiments on the Evil and Wicked Traffic of the Slavery and Commerce of the Human Species* (published in 1787). Clearly there was a more vigorous clash of ideas about "the human" than those we find in Behn or Defoe. What we find in their fictions are the outcomes, the resolutions, of that clash—the ideas that prevailed through the force of state and commerce, and that made their way by synthesis into the highest form of signification, the literary production of fiction.

Meanwhile, in their non-fiction texts, Sancho and Cugoana were outlining both the economic benefit and the ethical failure that produced the condition of slavery. One letter by Ignatius Sancho is written to the author of *Tristram Shandy*, Laurence Sterne. In it, Sancho compliments Sterne and the writer Sarah Scott for being among the few who paid attention to the anti-human horrors of slavery. It reads in part:

TO MR. STERNE. July, 1776. REVEREND SIR,

"Consider slavery—what it is—how bitter a draught—and how many millions are made to drink it!"—Of all my favourite authors, not one has drawn a tear in favour of my miserable black brethren—excepting yourself, and the humane author of Sir George Ellison.—I think you will forgive me;—I am sure you will applaud me for beseeching you to give one half-hour's attention to slavery, as it is at this day practised in our West Indies.— That subject, handled in your striking manner, would ease the yoke (perhaps) of many;—but if only of one— Gracious God!—what a feast to a benevolent heart!—and, sure I am, you are an Epicurean in acts of charity.—You, who are universally read, and as universally admired—you could not fail.—Dear Sir, think in me you behold the uplifted hands of thousands of my brother Moors.—Grief (you pathetically observe) is eloquent;—figure to yourself their attitudes;—hear their supplicating addresses!— Alas!—you cannot refuse.—Humanity must comply—in which hope I beg permission to subscribe myself,

> Reverend Sir, &c.
> IGN. SANCHO.[115]

Throughout the seventeenth and eighteenth centuries London had a thriving Black population, and by 1772, when Quobna Ottobah Cugoano arrived there, Black people made up two percent of the population. Many people who had been abducted and brought to England from various colonies escaped their abductors using the supposition that slavery had no "legal basis" in England. Cugoano was one such person, having escaped slavery when brought from Grenada to London by the man who claimed to be his owner. Cugoana then became an abolitionist, and the title of his treatise clarifies for us (if we retain the doubts that later propaganda produced) what he took for granted: that he saw slavery as criminal and its justifications as self-serving and base.

But it would be needless to arrange an history of all the base treatment which the African Slaves are subjected to, in order to shew the exceeding wickedness and evil of that insidious traffic, as the whole may easily appear in every part, and at every view, to be wholly and totally inimical to every idea of justice, equity, reason and humanity. What I intend to advance against that evil, criminal and wicked traffic of enslaving men, are only some Thoughts and Sentiments which occur to me, as being obvious from the Scriptures of Divine Truth, or such arguments as are chiefly deduced from thence, with other such observations as I have been able to collect. Some of these observations may lead into a larger field of consideration, than that of the African Slave Trade alone; but those causes from wherever they originate, and become the production of slavery, the evil effects produced by it, must shew that its origin and source is of a wicked and criminal nature . . .

However, it cannot but be very discouraging to a man of my complexion in such an attempt as this, to meet with the evil aspersions of some men, who say, "That an African is not entitled to any competent degree of knowledge, or capable of imbibing any sentiments of probity; and that nature designed him for some inferior link in the chain, fitted only to be a slave." But when I meet with those who make no scruple to deal with the human species, as with the beasts of the earth, I must think them not only brutish, but wicked and base; and that their aspersions are insidious and false: And if such men can boast of greater degrees of knowledge, than any African is entitled to, I shall let them enjoy all the advantages of it unenvied, as I fear it consists only in greater share of infidelity, and that of a blacker kind than only skin deep.[116]

What if this were the archive from which fictions were, and might be, imagined? I suppose what I am asking is: What if fictions were not written from those moments where, as Michel-Rolf Trouillot says, silence enters the archives of the history-making machines? Or rather, when we consider fictions, why reproduce those power relations unremarked—thereby engaging with notions of the human that were already being challenged, notions that were already being undone? How might one write fictions that are investigations, elaborations, of the dynamics of the arguments *in their time*—works that admit into their orbit-of-imagining the existence and the powerful influence of the writing of formerly enslaved abolitionists like Cugoano and Sancho? What if their texts and their accounts of encounters mattered in a way that produced a different kind of emplotment, and a rejection of the subject named as human?

VII. this paragraph is about a horse

As the horse continued in name, as well as fact, the property of Edmund, Mrs. Norris could tolerate its being for Fanny's use; and had Lady Bertram ever thought about her own objection again, he might have been excused in her eyes for not waiting till Sir Thomas's return in September, for when September came Sir Thomas was still abroad, and without any near prospect of finishing his business. Unfavourable circumstances had suddenly arisen at a moment when he was beginning to turn all his thoughts towards England; and the very great uncertainty in which everything was then involved determined him on sending home his son, and waiting the final arrangement by himself. Tom arrived safely, bringing an excellent account of his father's health; but to very little purpose, as far as Mrs. Norris was concerned.

—Jane Austen, *Mansfield Park*

This paragraph from Jane Austen's *Mansfield Park* is about a horse—specifically, the peccadillo of procuring a horse for Fanny Price without the consent of the lord of the house, Sir Thomas. But look at what follows, at what seems the only, slight impediment to the procurement of this "horse." "He wrote in April, and had strong hopes of settling everything to his entire satisfaction, and leaving Antigua before the end of the summer." Look at the freight that the horse carries—freight that we must nonetheless ignore, because our concern is for Fanny getting a horse, Edmund

Bertram's kindness, Mrs. Norris's meanness, Lady Bertram's distraction, Tom's safe arrival. Sir Thomas is in Antigua taking care of urgent matters still unexplained—but we are reading about a "horse" for Fanny.

If you are a reader like me, you wonder at the "unfavourable circumstances" and the "very great uncertainty." If you are a reader like me, "the final arrangement" grabs your attention, as does the laissez-faire way that the horse is made to bear it. If you are a reader like me, the five or so chapters about the young people of Mansfield Park staging a play are of absolutely no interest, and the puzzle of who loves whom never overpowers or satisfies the lacuna of "Antigua." If you are a reader like me, you may not have noticed this mention of Antigua until quite late in your reading, though the length and tediousness of the work may have made your eyes cross—especially then, in university. And the pleasure you understood to be the "normal" response, you pretended to have this then, too—well, you even *experienced* this pleasure, because it was supposed to be had. On this reader's part there was an odd patronizing in the false appreciation of these tedious passages. When one really wanted to say *who cares about this fatuousness*, one said *oh how great*. When the professor pointed out some pun or turn of phrase as evidence of the depth of the work, one gave him the point just to bear the instruction.

In *Mansfield Park* one notices the unearned erudition of the young characters; one notices that twenty-year-olds sound like they are forty. And one notices the too-much dialogue. But this is also the bequest of nineteenth-century literature, a bequest that makes twentieth- and twenty-first-century editors and professors demand dialogue from writers and find a book wanting if there is none.

One notices that every mention of the return of Sir Thomas Bertram, who had gone away to Antigua, contains a sense of dread—and one wonders if this was the unconscious speaking. "November was the black month fixed for his return," we are told, and, a little later on, we find the characters "lamenting over such an unlooked for premature arrival as a most untoward event, and without mercy wishing poor Sir Thomas had been twice as long on his passage, or were still in Antigua."[117]

The casual references to Antigua in the first half of the novel are sometimes made with a word or two of urgent meaning.

> . . . . Sir Thomas found it expedient to go to Antigua himself, for the better arrangement of his affairs, and he took his eldest son with him, in the hope of detaching him from some bad connexions at home. They left England with the probability of being nearly a twelve-month absent.

> . . . . His business in Antigua had latterly been prosperously rapid, and he came directly from Liverpool, having had an opportunity of making his passage thither in a private vessel, instead of waiting for the packet. . . .[118]

This looming without looming, this something going on in the wings, unseen, is what attracts this reader's attention. For it is something to do with the wealth accumulated at Mansfield

Park, "the pecuniary light" which Antigua casts on the five-mile surrounds and its modern-built house. It is this wealth, ease, taste and well-being that are the perquisites of Antigua and that business in Antigua. As Edward Said writes in *Culture and Imperialism*: "The Bertrams could not have been possible without the slave trade, sugar, and the colonial planter class; as a social type Sir Thomas would have been familiar to eighteenth- and early-nineteenth-century readers who knew the powerful influence of the class through politics, plays (like Cumberland's *The West Indian*)."[119] As Gikandi writes, "I suggest that the institutions of high culture in the English eighteenth century were enabled by money in the West Indian plantations."[120] Even in the last chapters, which are filled with the family shame and scandal of a married daughter running off with a rake, it is this wealth that is remarked upon. And while reputation and "love" may be lost, the materials of slavery bolster the disappointments, and can, in the case of Susan and Fanny, bring both hope and relief.

Equally of no interest to this reader are the four or five flatulent chapters about a ball for Fanny—until we come to Sir Thomas. He returns to interrupt the staging of the play, and advocates for a coming out ball, describing those that took place in Antigua— or rather, the narrator says that he describes them, but we are afforded no detail.

When the daughter—the "adulterer" Maria, who brings shame to the family—is sent with her aunt, Mrs. Norris, to "an establishment being formed for them in another country, remote and private," a reader like me wonders if this country might be Antigua. Yet Antigua is no country. To paraphrase John Stuart

Mill, as quoted in Said—or even better, to call "Antigua" in the terms of what George Lamming called the length and breadth of the Caribbean—it is a "site intended for production."[121]

The weight of greed and immoral thought in the novel is borne by Miss Crawford, who had her eyes on Edmund, the second and virtuous son of Sir Thomas. But to this reader she is the most honest character in her exchanges and letters about the stakes of the world of the novel. She will have Edmund if he inherits, and if he can be persuaded to see the world baldly, as she does. She is a perfect incarnation—one with the veneer of charm, money, desirability and cunning speech. *Mansfield Park* is considered a novel about morals, rightness and good conduct. But this reader sees that any character who honestly reminds the novel of its world is dispatched with and branded as being without virtue.

Said says, "My contention is that by that very odd combination of casualness and stress, Austen reveals herself to be assuming (just as Fanny assumes, in both senses of the word) the importance of an empire to the situation at home." I agree, and my contention is that the casualness is indeed casual, not intentional but reflexive—as casual as the state of knowledge, the state of living. It is nothing but a statement of relation, in its casualness. But I stop at the thought that *Mansfield Park* is a novel of "aesthetic intellectual complexity."[122] We attach these ascriptions to works many years after their creation, through the very long and insistent processes of empire that cause them to arrive as objects of aesthetic value. Even more, there are social processes that assign aesthetic value to visual and textual objects, processes that have to do with systems of ruling. How is a Gucci logo bag beautiful? It really isn't. It's only Gucci. Why is a Louis Vuitton logo bag beautiful and desirable? It is repetitive and unremarkable; it signals wealth, not beauty. Its stamp signals class, acquisition, desire, extraction and a sameness. A paper bag is more beautiful.

Mansfield Park is long and flabby—and I know what those many pages meant in the economies of publishing of the time, and in the bourgeois-making project contained in the economies of reading at the time, too. There may have been no doom scrolling then, but those economies had their own fatuousness. They had their own ways of time wasting, just as we do in the present—or, rather, the same seduction and hold of attending to capital. It was just beginning then, the metropolitan grasping, the greed for "things," and the sublimating or obfuscating of whatever provided the path toward acquiring them.

Mansfield Park was published 126 years after Aphra Behn's *Oroonoko*, 95 years after Daniel Defoe's *The Adventures of Robinson Crusoe*. Through these novels, one cannot refuse to observe the genealogy and the longevity of the European imperialist aesthetic. Yet these texts insist on our attention, our fealty. They are reproduced on television and in movies over and over; they are reproduced by modern writers of all genres, reinforcing the aesthetic of this system of ideas.

For readers like us—the two women photographed in front of the library some years ago, the one in the mini-skirt with the books in her hand, the other in the denim jacket and bell-bottoms with the green bag—this paragraph is not about a horse at all. Readers like us read the world of the paragraph, its desires, its decisions, its assumptions, its relation, its perpendicularities.

This aesthetic is what readers like us, alert in the sensorium of catastrophe produced by that world from which those novels emanated, recognize as the problem. I am not interested in the morality of any given writer; I am interested in the construction of, and the information contained in and relayed by, their paragraphs. I want to see what the writing imports from the systems in which the writer (and the work) is immersed—the social relations and political aspirations it, and they, spring from.

An autobiography of interruption, but much more

I. sound

As insidious as England was during my childhood, so was America. While no one that we—those children in that early photograph—knew had gone there yet, America was invading, had invaded. It was a seemingly less ascetic imperialism, with a less strict aesthetic; an aesthetic, in fact, suggesting some license, some liberty of expression, a suaveness, a likeability—these were its contours. The USA, or America as it was familiarly called, presented a contestation with the stiff upper lip of Britain. And what America did was take over the sound of the landscape. If Britain ruled the schools and the formalities of life, America seeped into the spaces less locked down by those colonial arrangements. If the morning radio was filled with Britain—the dispatches and news—the afternoon radio, and especially the Saturday radio, was filled with America. As the boats became airplanes, as technology was expanded and varied, America arrived fully in our cognition. As the waning of one empire gave way to the next, America grew in importance in our lives. Never quite replacing England, such was the cultural power of the British Empire, but rivalling and filling the economic and cultural spaces.

One might say that America arrived as the antidote to Britain. One did not have to knock one's head against its great books, its long tradition of literature, dominant and irremovable; one only had to listen to its sound. That sound came with its own imperial project—and its level of pleasure lent even more effectiveness to its influence. Sound is a more visceral lector. It enters the body seemingly unbidden, casually. It consists of vibrations that travel through air. Its work is to permeate the air, to saturate the body. And music, music does this most of all. It adds structure to sound. Memorable and retrievable, it can gather time. So, the long car-sick childhood rides back and forth from San Fernando to Guayaguayare, through Usine Ste. Madeleine, Princes Town, Indian Walk, New Grant, Tableland, Fonrose, Poole, Rio Claro, Mafeking, Ortoire, Mayaro, Grand Lagoon were immanent with the sound of Jim Reeves's "Am I Losing You," "He'll Have to Go," "This World Is Not My Home," "Adios Amigo," "I Love You Because" and on and on. (And why do I remember unbidden that he died in a plane crash when I was eleven, and how this added to his song's delivery?) Connie Francis's "Who's Sorry Now?" and "Everybody's Somebody's Fool" underpinned the ubiquitous Americanism. The thought of and the recall of these songs now fills me with deep sadness, the kind of piercing mournfulness which was their register. And also a slender revulsion, a respiratory spasm at the long effects. They summon for me the idea of wasted or interrupted emotional attention, of wasted, disturbed time. Just like the British books I read, the American songs dragged one's thoughts away and intimated again that our existence was one not worth conceiving. Sound has the quality of duration; even when not immediate, a song is present and its effects can seemingly be fully reprised: the day you heard it, where you were, the events of that day into which the sound interpolated. If you were a child, with only the events of the life of the adults in the family as your focus, then their lives were, on that day, as you see it, struck through by the sound. Even as complicated as the lives themselves already are, furcated by public colonial exigencies and private granular concurrences, this sound, the sound of America, now intervenes/ed. America was replacing Britain as the imperialist power in the world. It was less concerned with the everyday deportment of its subjects than with the laissez-faire control of all their resources. Its aesthetic would be the commodification of everything, the acquisition of everything.

My grandmother, my aunts, my uncles, the taxi driver Dillon, the shopkeeper Lloyd, the schoolteacher Mrs. Shand—they all loved these songs. The boy and girl next door and the boy across the street loved these songs, and we would run outside to play hopscotch belting out "Adios Amigo" or "Somebody's Fool," ingesting their far-away-ness, their sophistication, their whiteness, there elsewhere-ness, their America. America's reputation was outlaw. Its films were about outlaws or impropriety, and they "buried themselves in our chests."[123] Its speech, at least the sound of its speech, was to us outlaw, not proper. It drawled. In the sound of its movies, the actors whined, they were nasal, their speech was drawn out and slow. The most iconic character was the outlaw; and the outlaw most deeply and irrevocably embedded in the Western movie was the gunslinger. The righteous killer of "Indians." This figure travelled five thousand kilometres to a backyard in San Fernando, Trinidad—first on the radio, then in the comic books, then on the screen. The Lone Ranger.

Tonto. The at once docile and hostile Indigenous figure remained the same as in the British novels we read, and we children were invited to enact this whiteness in another medium, with new hosts. We did not have a television at first, but we looked through our window into the neighbours' window, peering at their television. When we did get our own TV, we were glued to whiteness in the visual.

These phantasms, visual and auditory, caused dreadful envy and identification in us, so far away and longing for something not-British, not of England, not of those colonial strictures. Bing Crosby's "The Christmas Song" begins, "Chestnuts roasting on an open fire . . ."; it may have been the most insipid and damaging of these imperializing songs. The lyrics, altogether inane, moved from the whitewashing of a particular northern American landscape to the paternalistic monolith of a capitalistic patriarchal fantasy. What is it to sit in your living room with its shiny floor, its Morris chairs, its dish cabinet, its window allowing the beautiful sun in, its door to the verandah wide open, the birds singing, the smell of black cake from the kitchen, and the smell of roasted ham, the laughter of your aunt, the one who took you to Mr. Wong's studio, her always-golden laughter, the expectation of guests, and then to hear from the radio or the record player Bing Crosby singing, "Jack Frost nipping at your nose . . ."? You are hailed by envy for some environment in which it would be better to enjoy this season and celebration. You are reminded of the simulacra of your life experience. Then you talk of what it will be like when you go to that place; what it must or will feel like. Your experience of the world is latent. And then the living room becomes a waiting room, an airport, a train station, a boat.

Bing Crosby's avuncular, slightly smarmy sound compounds the already problematic Christianity the season celebrates. (At least the myth of Christ being born under difficult conditions is one you can sympathize with; it bears some resemblance to the general condition in which you live.)

The whole exercise induced distraction. We drifted away from a possible self that might have been recognizable in our social and historical conditions, and in our physical presences; we discarded that self and inhaled the fantasies of whiteness and capital. One felt distracted, attending to this new regime of observances and lessons. It applied a certain pressure; it moved at a certain velocity. It was another preoccupation, it was another direction to turn toward. So, it is worth remarking its arrival as sound—as the force of air particles vibrating against each other, moving quickly, enveloping the atmosphere.

Then on Sunday—or was it Saturday?—Billy Graham's ominous *The Hour of Decision* came on the air. This dreaded hour included a singer, George Beverly Shea, who sang "I Go Along the Road Praising the Lord." And another singer, Cliff Barrows, who sang "What a Friend We Have in Jesus." The sound was quite frightening and still is now—a choral belligerence, a loud insistent bellowing. At the time, for my grandmother and the household, it was another attachment to the righteous. If the Anglican church on Harris Promenade adhered to an asceticism because it required the proper dress, the proper tithe, at least Graham's evangelism could bawl its discourses through the living room.

The songs we heard dominating the airwaves closed the horizon of imagination and condemned the landscape. If you listened to Jim Reeves singing "This World Is Not My Home" as you wilted in the back seat of Mr. Dillon's car with your sisters and your cousins, a lime in your hand for motion sickness, you would understand this sound's malevolence. Out of the car window the passing fields grew irrelevant; the sharp cane stalks were superseded as "here." And if the dreadful news that *this world is not my home* is true, you wondered tearfully, then where is? A deep alienation infected you.

I once wrote in a poem, "We believed in nothing / The black and white American movies buried themselves in our chests / liquid glacial, acidic as love."[124] It was the sound of America that interred us after the British Empire declined somewhat in our lives. First came the radio; later came the movies elaborating the sound in image.

Speech itself, the rules of standard British English against the demotic—language itself—was deeply contested and policed then. Somewhere deep in the everyday, but as yet unsanctioned, was the insurgent music of steel pan and calypso, which had its own internal battle with race and class. This, even as the burgeoning anti-colonialism admitted every day, more and more, a Black nationalism. Those cultural expressions would eventually breach this sound of America—breach and overwhelm, thankfully. It took the voluminous, original and orchestral sound of "pan"—a communal and sonorous sound from the working class—to overwhelm American sound. In fact, it would take the invention of a new instrument—the steel pan, the only new percussive instrument invented in the twentieth century—to intervene, to return the interrupted, to contest the imperialist, to resist that "American" sound. In his book *The Illustrated Story of Pan*, music theorist Kim Johnson writes, "The operative principle underlying the music that Africans brought to the New World is that it must help people to live."[125] This is the sound, the imperative, of pan.

In C.L.R. James's *Minty Alley*, England and America appear together early on. The narrator describes the ambitions of the protagonist's mother for him: "In the West Indies, to get a profession meant going to England or America, and his mother had decided she would send him to England. She was a headmistress and in her spare time taught unwearyingly. First, she had bought the house on a stiff mortgage. Haynes was to work in the island for a year or two and then, when the mortgage had been paid off, she would send him abroad and keep him there."[126]

But Haynes's mother dies, and Haynes moves into a rooming house at 2 Minty Alley. It is owned by Mrs. Rouse, whose husband has abandoned her and gone to America with another woman. Haynes is a middle-class young man through whose eyes we witness the ups and downs of life in the working-class Minty Alley—the travails and intrigues of secret love lives, infidelities, financial hardship, striving, run-ins with the police and courts and bailiffs. Haynes has a relationship with Maisie, Mrs. Rouse's niece, who has every plan to get out of Minty Alley and travel to America. "But she wanted to go to America to work for good money. In America you worked hard but you got good food and pay and had a fine time. Why the hell should she starve and slave to get a few shillings a week from some employer in the town?"[127]

At the end of the novel, after a nasty fight with her aunt, Maisie leaves on a boat for New York City. Without any substantial money, Maisie manages to do this by guile and scheme, as she describes to Haynes:

> "But the stewardess on the _____ line has an assistant and sometimes two. And if you pay her twenty dollars you get the job. She has been after me a long time."
>
> "Why after you?"
>
> "She likes to get young coloured girls who are nice. The white officers like them."
>
> "So you mean, Maisie—"
>
> "Mr. Haynes. I want a job and I am going to get it. The captain and the whole crew can't get anything from me unless I want to give them. The boat is in and if I get the job I am going. You have papers to sign that you are coming back. But when that boat hit New York and I put my foot on shore, if it wait for me before it leave, it's going to wait a damned long time."
>
> "So everything's fixed, Maisie."
>
> "Everything, Mr. Haynes."
>
> There was a harshness and determination behind the casual air with which she spoke that stunned him into acceptance.[128]

By the end of *Minty Alley*, America is the direction of all ambitions.

But another sound arrived, one that cut through and eventually superseded that white sound. It carried the insurgent

anti-colonial Black nationalism. My aunts, my uncles, my grandmother and grandfather, the entire neighbourhood, loved Ella
Fitzgerald and Sarah Vaughan. They loved Dinah Washington
singing "This Bitter Earth," "I Wanna Be Loved" and "Teach Me
Tonight." If I hear those songs now, I am taken away with a
deep pleasure. I can see my childhood living room and hear my
aunts' laughter. They loved Billy Eckstine's smooth, deep, elegant vibrato singing "What Kind of Fool Am I?" These singers
were respite. Across the street at my neighbours', Ivan, one of
two brothers, would play his saxophone every afternoon after
work, practicing Lester Young's "There Will Never be Another
You." He never played in public, he only practised. I don't think
he ever perfected the song. This part of America, Black America,
the part that would thankfully become America's only distinc-
tive sound, is one my family, my street, recognized and identified
with. This sound bestowed a sophistication, and a knowledge
that other Black people inhabited this "away," that they lived
at the source of this new imperialism—and this knowledge was
a source of comfort, however troubled. We knew that those
Black people struggled too, and yet, like us they created a sound.
It was aspirational.

This is an affinity that Richard Wright points to and sum-
marises in his 1953 introduction to George Lamming's *In The
Castle of My Skin:*

> Even before Lamming leaves his island home, that home
> is already dying in his heart; and what happens to
> Lamming after that is something that we all know, for we
> have but to lift our eyes and look into the streets and we

see countless young, dark-skinned Lammings of the soil marching in picket lines, attending political rallies, impulsively, frantically seeking a new identity. . . . Just as young Lamming is ready to leave Barbados Island for Trinidad, Trumper, who has gone to America and has been influenced by mass racial and political agitation, returns and, in a garbled manner, tells of the frenzied gospel of racial self-assertion—that strange soul-food of the rootless outsiders of the twentieth century. The magnetic symbol of Paul Robeson (shown here purely in racial and *not* political terms!) attracts as much as disturbs young Lamming as he hears Robeson sing over a tiny recording device: Let My People Go![129]

My uncle loved Nat King Cole. To us he even looked like Nat King Cole, a resemblance that gave him a brief cachet, although he could not sing. Nat King Cole's version of "The Christmas Song" was urbane—it seemed satiric, or ironic, and it rendered the earlier Bing Crosby version simplistic and insincere. It was of another intellectual order, and that contradiction layered all the contradictions already present. Like Maisie in *Minty Alley*, people thought they simply had to get there, they only had to "jump the ship" as Maisie planned to do, and they would be able to handle the rest, in America. They would do anything to get their "feet caught in the sweet flypaper of life."[130]

II. this paragraph is about a town

Dawson's Landing was a slaveholding town, with a rich, slave-worked grain and pork country back of it. The town was sleepy and comfortable and contented. It was fifty years old, and was growing slowly—very slowly, in fact, but still it was growing.

Early in the tale *Pudd'nhead Wilson*, by Mark Twain, published in 1894, past the descriptions of landscape where the action of the novel takes place, past the set-up of rose plants, hollyhocks, honeysuckle and pretty homes, the above-quoted paragraph appears. We have been prepared for this paragraph with the idyllic folksy gestures of flowers and rivers. Very often in my experience of reading I have encountered such a paragraph, a paragraph of contradictory sentences. *The town was sleepy and comfortable and contented.* Amazing. Always amazing to me. What about the enslaved of the previous sentence? They apparently did not constitute the town, and how interesting is the state of affairs that had to be elided to open the tale—a fact of incredible importance had to be made passive, to be rid of its violence, in order to continue elocuting. And what a modifying compound word, *slave-worked*. The second sentence must pacify the first so that the tale may continue in that register of contentment, comfort and sleep. "Dawson's landing was a slaveholding town, with a rich, slave-worked grain and pork country back of it." The second sentence having cauterized the first, we are invited to view what proceeds, to judge what proceeds from this benign vantage point. We are invited to locate our sympathies and our expectations in the second sentence's investment. We will attend to the characters plucked out by the author from the first sentence. We will attend to the characters plucked out by the author, not from the slave-worked back of it but from the intimate spaces of the slaveholding town. That is, we will attend to the intimate or domestic space of the white people of the town. In this intimate or domestic space, there are enslaved Black people who may or may not work also in the slave-worked back of it, but who also work in and around the white household. The narrative is of course about the exchanging of babies, the exchanging of racially indistinguishable babies by the enslaved Roz to protect her child from being sold away. And this is where Pudd'nhead Wilson, lawyer and early adopter of the new technology of fingerprints, comes into it. But this is unimportant in my assessment of this paragraph; it is only another obfuscation in plot that does more of the same work, burying the contradictions of the paragraph or, perhaps, illustrating them. It is illustrating, perhaps, the white world's nonchalance about slavery as a breakage with the concept of human freedom, a concept that underlies all the desires of the white world yet is withheld from the livingness of others. The novel, despite the many characters and dramatic situations the first sentence suggests, settles on the interplay inside the white household.

So, the author chooses "domestic" slaves, those slaves who work in the house, as his sub-protagonists, falsely implying a benign relation, presenting the part for the whole and eliding the massive enslaved agricultural labour. As if slavery was a "domestic" inconvenience, the enslaved merely the instruments of whiteness or white accomplishment or white actuation, and the figures of the enslaved merely incorrigible puppets, not an exploited and brutalized labour force upon which the economic viability of comfort, contentment and sleep depends. A structural problem of English literary narrative allows this sleight of hand, since all we must be concerned about is the individual plight, the individual striving against "life's" odds. This is the idyll that soothes the reader—as if the antagonism is personal and not social/structural, as if the appraisal of a state of being involves one individual instead of the mass of individuals who come under the regime. I would say that this novel, and all of Twain generally, regularized a certain view of the enslaved, and consequently of blackness as "domestic" terrain. And it is the single protagonist that accomplishes this domesticating of the historical. The historical sweep is reduced to the personal, the domestic. To "personalize" or atomize the tale by creating a single protagonist in the world, or a protagonist energized, underwritten by, made intrinsic by, individualism, leaches that tale of its global significance. Perhaps when the world of European contact comes into being, this atomization comes along with it—and this style of narration becomes the purview, the terrain of the colonizer. Meanwhile, in truth, narration is no longer possible, if it ever was, in any form other than the multivocal for the colonized.

The language of the novel, the supposed affectation of the speech and colloquialisms of the time, assaulted me in university. The derogatory nomenclature in the text was supposed to represent the folksy—the taken-for-granted. We, whom the gratuitous words attacked, were supposed to understand works like these as literature. We were asked to cordon off the effects of literature while lauding the effects of literature. This whole racial assault we were supposed to take with equanimity, or with a good-natured quality. If we did not, it was as if we could not take a joke—or could not take the truth.

Published in 1901, seven years after *Pudd'nhead Wilson*, Charles Chesnutt's novel *The Marrow of Tradition* is in many ways a rejoinder to Twain's novel. It identifies as "marrow" the white supremacist core of Twain's narration. And it is a correction to the sport that Twain makes of Black people, his playing around with "character" and questions of "nature" versus "nurture." *Marrow* is an urgent response to the Wilmington Race Riot in 1898, in which hundreds of the Black residents of Wilmington, North Carolina were murdered, and the remainder driven out in what was the only (or one of the only) successful insurrections in the US. *The Marrow of Tradition*, too, centres on a town—in this instance, Wellington, North Carolina. It is a town where the white former slave owners and overseers think that the Black population is enjoying too much freedom, post-slavery.

While in Twain there is no antagonism—he creates a folksy though sly sketch—Chesnutt rips aside the veil on Black suffering; he exposes white mendacity and violence. Working in many of the same materials around law, around nature and nurture, Chesnutt's novel is not set in an idyllic slave past that never existed but in the lead-up to a violent pogrom against Black residents. Chesnutt refuses the folksy domesticated individualist narrative. Wellington is another town altogether, a town in which the white residents are belligerent, and the Black residents are trying to make a way, sometimes enjoying themselves while navigating white hostility with clearly understood performances of subservience. Wellington is a town on the brink of manufactured rage against the Black inhabitants, which soon leads to an insurrection in which hundreds of the Black residents are murdered and most of the rest driven out.

There are intrigues in Chesnutt's novel that feature disinheritance, bad blood, doubles (Janet Miller and Olivia Carteret, Tom Delamere and Sandy) and legal escapades. But the feeling is different when one reads Chesnutt. Chesnutt is not having fun at the expense of Black people; he is not laughing at them. Rather, he alerts us to the ways in which it is the sound of Black laughter, and the fact of Black people living outside of subservience, that enrages the white townspeople. The sound of Black laughter, of Black enjoyment, activates deadly white resentment. In contrast, my contention is that Twain's *Pudd'nhead Wilson* has absolutely nothing to do with Black people. What it expresses is whiteness and its disaffection with humanity.

The books, the sounds, the images; Britain, America, empires—these all arrived as the universal, into which we were supposed to climb. We immediately recognized that we were supposed to become that universal—and also that this was an aspirational category, not a given condition. We would strive to become this universal while recognizing we were not part of it, even as we received lifelong sentences to be advocates for our own entry. We understood the grandiosity of the call and its limits and borders, but we who were "educated" were supposed to become that universal through our own diligent application—or, as it turns out, by a miracle; or no, by self-delusion.

A sense of interruption is the pervading quality of this reading/ seeing life: something like a self being interrupted; something like an alternative life being foreclosed, although interruption is different from foreclosure. Interruption is ongoing; it has shorter and continuous, or consecutive, time lapses. What is being interrupted is opaque to you. You have received the thing undone, like a set of minute parts of something recognizable. Interruption is something physical but also about duration—it could gather itself, but each effort to do so meets with more interruption.

It is unbearable for me to watch any television show or popular film about Black people within the framework of the capitalist-machine-making of images of blackness. Those are the scenes of the deepest interruption because those are the scenes where a promise of self-observation, of "characterization," is offered and withdrawn quite commonsensically. I say "commonsensically" because all representations within this machine take the capitalist form, and even when these images supposedly resist, inevitably they must assimilate into the form. Traditional films—that is, films in which whiteness is the organizing logic— invariably show Black people as desirous of entering capital, that is to say, whiteness; as sellers of themselves as commodity, that is to say, blackness. Which is further to say: desirous of obtaining the position of whiteness. This desire, to exchange blackness for whiteness (and its travails), is considered a good quest for the character, and that quest is at the base of many such films. The Black character must pass the test of showing that they are not commodity. It is considered a worthy ambition to enter capital, thereby signifying that one is not a commodity. That is, that one is not Black. It is on this value that the character succeeds or fails.

The films propose that Black characters are commodity, saleable, without an ethical footing. The schema is this: enter as commodity because you are marked as commodity, then play out the drama of the commodity seeking to be capital/ist. This is the Sisyphean arc of Black characterization.

Black writers too, often must prove the "universality" of the experiences they write. They are charged with facilitating a transparency of experience, and this experience must be delivered in the register of stereotype. That is, for the Black writer and putative subject, "universality" often means that the life they describe be done in the terms of Euro-American understanding—which may, in fact, be counter to, and contradictory of, the lived life. In other words, they are often charged with reproducing stereotypes commensurate with those already understood from the consecrated texts of the Euro-American tradition. The interpretive field of Black life in white discourse is meagre. To refuse the fixed recitation, to wander freely through experience, time and space, is to breach the boundary of the required transparency.

III. vestiges: to look again

I have been trying to think of how one is made and how one makes oneself. I have been thinking that one is made through events—historical, familial, known and unknown; one is made also by what one reads, by what one experiences—all this underpins how one comes to know oneself; and one is made through the action, realization and analysis that constructs a self. One is made, too, by what Michel-Rolph Trouillot names as silence and power in the production of history.

One is made by works of literature, and one is made through and by narrative. Or, rather, I have been made, and continue to be made, in and by literature. A photograph taken of me when I was about four years old opens a narrative world. It is a source of endless readings, endless looking. It has become artifact—an object of cultural or historical significance that one studies and theorizes because of its unknowability, because of its existence in another time.

I call this section "To Look Again" so as to examine a photograph as vestige and see how it generated, in the end, a novel, a poem, a set of thinking. I want to look again, to afford, to allow interpretation of the materials of life—"a" life, a common life, a life in the historical, a life in the act of living. A life in the act of narrative-making, and life at the level of narrative.

"To look again" is to try to make sense of that act of living, to illuminate that which, though felt at cellular level, could not be seen or fully understood in the immediate. In that photograph taken when I was perhaps four, was I living everything to follow? If the photograph captured time, can time's duration be seen in it? I mean time not as destiny, but as possibility, as matter. Destiny has a closed narrative shape, it is a told tale, but time is much more suggestive. To look again means to try to unravel what simultaneity, or the brutal efficiencies of domination, obscures and collapses; to bring new knowledge, or knowledge that one had no access to at the time, to bear on past (ongoing) events. Certainly, something was predictable from the photograph. But not everything. To look again is to reassess the act of living through a process of critical understanding and transformation—in other words, to upend and affect certain ways of thinking, certain ways of knowing and certain ways of being in the world; it is to negate certain scripts. This is the beautiful thing that time affords and afforded the girls in the photograph.

So let me use that photograph again. Read it again. Look at it again. Here I will use that photograph to talk about its traces and trajectories through writing, and through my novel, *At the Full and Change of the Moon*. That novel was my clearest attempt, I now see, to describe the photograph in total, in the way that fiction might. That is, to describe what came before and what came after, what placed the girl/s in that moment in Mr. Wong's studio, and the photograph's many elaborations. The photograph from my childhood has always been and still is a mystery to me, or an opening, a wonder, and a source of inexhaustible looking. And writing. And so it is possible that everything since, and therefore my writing life, emanates from the photograph. Why? Because the photograph narrates and is a record of my world at four as it collides with apprehension. The photograph's survival attests to its significance. Very few photographs mark this period in my family. This photograph is the surviving family portrait. The four cousins, or the three children and their cousin, or the child and her three cousins, or the girl, her two sisters, and her cousin, or the eldest girls of the family. Or . . .

I think that by the time this work is done, perhaps the photograph will disappear as a physical object—dissolved or oxidized by looking again. Or, perhaps, the photograph will look different. It will be populated fully and visibly by all the spectres of its generation. Every figure not in the direct focus of the photographer, Mr. Wong, comes into view for me when I look at the photograph again. Just as looking at an artifact makes visible all its human coordinates.

To complicate matters, I want now to use the photo as an autobiography, in the specific way that Antonio Gramsci conceived autobiography as "the smallest unit of analysis capable of understanding subject and object caught in the processes of biological and historical change."[131] Autobiography, as he proposed, may expose the relation between individual and collective formation. And though I did not take the photograph—so in a pure sense it is biographical, since it is authored by the photographer—it is still an attempt by me to authorize and comport a particular kind of subject. I feel that I was complicit enough in its making, even though I was four years old, to call it autobiography. I helped to make the photograph by looking into the camera, by helping Mr. Wong arrange, or pacify, my sister with that blur of a rattle, and by reaching out with my sudden awareness to the world beyond the photograph. The photograph has come to be incorporated in how I/we/the subjects know our/my "self"—it is simultaneously "here I am / we are" and "there we are / I am." When I ask my sisters to look at the photograph, they see themselves. I do not see me, though I see me looking out of the photograph. And I recall not merely following Mr. Wong's instruction but feeling responsible to the project of the photograph. That is probably too wild a claim—so fictional—nevertheless.

I want to employ the photograph in all these ways, as a unit of analysis showing a family in a certain time under certain circumstances, but also a family being made within the history the photograph occurs inside and which it also elaborates, and within a moment when agency glimmers from the subjects in the frame.

From 1956/57 to 1965, we received blue airmail letters from my mother and my aunt every fortnight, containing the blurred news of their world and life. They never sent bad news about that life, only occasionally something of an apology, such as, "Sorry I am not able to send as much as I had hoped; please do with this until I can do better." They would look into the photograph, I imagine, knowing the difficult days contained within the preposition "until." This "until" we lived as scarcity, what we called "sweetwater days." They—my mother and aunt—lived in the world the photographer ushered our images into, the world that constructed the inabilities contained in the negative verb "not able." They, and England, would sustain our existence between that melancholic preposition and the adverse verb. The anxieties of our house/family would depend on the precarious promise of England. This photograph is the only photograph of my childhood, and it is incendiary with the occasion, the occurrence of England. There is no other reason for the existence of the photograph—no familial or whimsical or benign reason. As portentous as the photograph is, it exists in an administrative register.

The photograph is something of a passport to that place called England—an identity photograph. My mother and my aunt left home under the impression that they, too, must/will make a good appearance, as I said near the start of this work. These good appearances caused them to hide their intimate lives from their family back on the island. It is critically important that they did so, in order to send the remittances—that they *must* send—back to the family. Their only mission was to *do* better, not to "live." So, the hiding of those intimate lives must have cost them, did cost them. And we, the ones being photographed, must look toward/at them, assuring them that their experience is not in vain, that their memory of us, supported by this photograph, is vital—as in alive, as in necessary to their journey to England. They did not go to live lives, they went to work, to labour. My mother, returning ten years later, would say with rage, when facing some misdemeanour on our part, "I walked the streets of London with one dress on my back for you to behave like this to me?" In those moments one only heard the explosive and precarious, the pain and the restriction, of her extracted labour. And one can definitely imagine what other hardships she may have endured, though she was silent on those. At every other moment after returning, she represented London/England as her glory days—the elbow gloves she loved; the guipure lace dress folded delicately in her suitcase; the bangers and mash that she cooked on special and rare occasions when she seemed happy. My aunt's decades-long wistfulness for Tenerife, or the sight of Tenerife, leaps backward—to just *before* the arrival in

England. I might interpret that lacuna as full of the same unspoken hardship. Her legendary rectitude makes her declaration of wistfulness for Tenerife a surprising response.

We must look out into the camera, Mr. Wong says. "Little girls, smile! Don't cry." I recall trying to follow his instruction; my little sister is crying, and my cousin is trembling in sympathy. The effort of standing still with attention, and the unknown and unquantifiable expectations of the empty place beyond Mr. Wong, is too stressful. I must calm my cousin and my little sister. And I must also look out into the camera. *My older sister is aloof,* though now, I think, she seems sad, *with her own self-arrangement.* She, my older sister, will carry the weight of us in years to come, because she is the oldest. She will be instructed by my grandmother to go to all grocery stores, department stores, official buildings— and she will write all the letters to England. She will become a businesswoman, she will always be stylish; she will use this skill, the skill of self-arrangement, to move quickly from any bad moment to an optimism beyond any I could muster with my shaking toy rattle. I could not persuade my little sister not to cry, nor could I persuade my cousin not to be afraid. And I can't persuade anyone even now. The toy rattle is a blur in the photograph—it is only because I say that it is a toy rattle that makes it so; and I say it only because of my memory of that afternoon. It was a Saturday afternoon, I remember. It could only be a Saturday afternoon. The blur of the rattle must have some meaning—it is moving faster than the speed of the photographer's shutter. And, at the moment Mr. Wong takes the photograph, the rattle seems caught on the hem of my dress. My memory of the afternoon is what survives to tell me it is me in the photograph.

We will all go to England when we grow up. That is a certainty. That is the plan. England is a better place. *Our lives will revolve around and be decided in the sacred blue airmail letters sent and received.* We will turn the pages of the Harrods department store catalogue, outwitting each other to claim which things are ours—whoever's finger lands first on the image owns it: stoves, dresses, teapots, irons, shoes, combs, practical items, goods, a broom, a set of cutlery, a teacup—not merely toys, as one might expect, but materials, the products of the relations of the movement of goods and people—a brush, a tray, a suitcase, an ironing board. We will do this for all the years of our childhood. This catalogue will be our game when it is raining, the whole rainy season long. This book will be dog-eared and torn, especially if someone cheats. Then the others will grab the book and claim all of the products and vow never to play with the cheater again.

There we are, struggling for our best behaviour, wearing our best dresses, ribbons in our hair, our going-out shoes, the flowered linoleum of the studio floor, the beige curtain behind us. Is it that I am not anyone I will know after the photograph?

Mr. Wong arranged us not in terms of height or age but staggered, short, tall, short, tall. We could be any children there—so the photograph is in many ways quite ordinary, quite plain. It is meant to record, not disrupt. Any photograph in 1957 sent to England may have looked this way. This photographer, Mr. Wong, had taken many photos such as this one. My friends also took the finely dressed walk up McGillvary Street to send photos to someone in England. Up the street and down the Coffee—as the main street was called—toward Wong's studio on Lord Street, or was it Mucurapo Street? So, there are many photographs like this one. The photographs I will see later, making the opposite journey to the "colonies" from England, will have a contradictory look: a look of their past "us," and their new present "*they*" and "*there*"—a photograph with a telephone in their hand like a prop certifying wealth; or a photograph next to a car, a Vauxhall or a Bentley they were passing by, not one they owned but one they could imply that they owned. A photograph of a person wearing a tweed coat, an elbow glove, a cardigan. Next to a bicycle, next to a record player, next to a fireplace, down a posh street, at the window of a posh shop next to a red telephone booth. These photographs would contain an object then, a foreign object, signifying well-being and referencing the place: London, Manchester, Liverpool, Blackpool, England. There were other photos from England, similar to the ones we received, from similar studios in England with a similar linoleum, although the clothing was always richer—or richer in our view. These photographs would display a stylish disarray, yet there would be something inside the photograph that told of the effort—the effort to look at ease.

What is the disarray I read? The part of the subject that was still ours alongside the part of the subject being simultaneously surrendered and constructed, willingly. Or what is that unease I read? The racial work of the state pressing against the lens, and they, the subjects, clasping a few objects to compensate for their affective losses.

In contrast, the photographs of us that travelled north would not have these props, nor would they reference the conditions in which they were taken, only the hopes that were displayed through neatness and a presentation of good behaviour.

All the photos we received signalled a life abroad or a life addressing the metropole. They signalled arrival in what the West deemed the present. Any other kind of photograph, the ones like the photographs of us, the photographs being sent north to the metropole, became a kind of ethnographic portrait of a past or "primitive" time. We and they lived in the same time, but time is only measured by this address to modernity—some photographs lock time; some move time. So of course, I do not recognize myself. This unrecognizability is the disturbance that will return again and again—as curiosity, as investigation, as reading and writing what the photograph summons and unearths.

My mother sent us a photograph of herself in her midwife's uniform riding a bike somewhere in Croydon. It is a beautiful photograph of a young intense woman going about her affairs. The bicycle makes her look both carefree and serious. Is this why a bicycle appears with frequency in my poems and novels? When I look at that photograph years later, my mother doesn't look quite so carefree, but carefree and capable is my memory of the photograph. I never learned to ride a bicycle, but a bicycle keeps appearing in a stanza or a line I write.

My youngest aunt went to England later, in the sixties. There is no photograph of her, but there is a story and an image. It is an image of a brown coat, and a story of two dreary sisters who met her at the airport with that coat and a pair of brown boots. She hated the coat and the boots. And she hated the sight of blood, which made her vomit. So, Wandle Valley Hospital would be her destination only briefly. She had entered swinging London of the sixties and had to break away, which she did, from these sisters. When I next met her, we drank Camparis on the ferry from Dover to Ostend, going to where she lived in Zeebrugge.

A family photo is full of absences and presences. Perhaps photos, any kind of photos, are always full of absence and presence, particularly if you occupy the history of the New World and cannot trace yourself to the current victors. You see the "after" image and the "before" image. You see the preposition "*but.*" You see a layer of the image that is adjacent, or palimpsestic, to discourses of coloniality. The image is the sight and site that exposes the incendiary fissures, the eruptive imagination that may overturn coloniality. Even the personal photograph is historical—not in the sense of dating the photograph, as in saying *this photo was taken in 1957,* but as in: *this photo was taken when absences—the ascription of "colonial subjects"—were being consolidated in reference to modernity's presences.* And when particular absences were authorized so that a suitable subjectivity might be constituted.

If I read that photograph of the four girls as the making of the reading subject, and more importantly, here, the writing subject; if I take the photograph as a vector leading to my writing—I see that it was also a catalyst for narrating the world in front of the photograph, the world of and before the photograph, and the world after it. I see it as the eruption of presence and absence. The anxiety of the photo is the listening, attending girl in the photo—the girl in the photo who will not recognize herself after the photo. I recall the taking of the photograph as a kind of coming into the public for the "me" who is in the photo; a coming into the awareness of a public who had understandings and desires; an encounter with unknown people for whom one could not necessarily predict or assume desires or understandings. The occasion produced an awareness of myself as a consciousness in conversations with unknown consciousnesses. And it produced a looking subject—and, ultimately, an observing subject.

There are numberless anxieties in the photograph, as I read it now. Those histories that appear and disappear in the photograph prompted in me a curiosity about history and historiography— a curiosity that worked its way into fiction.

I will go with my sisters and cousin to an Anglican school. We will wear brown three-pleated uniforms with white blouses underneath. My older sister will guide us on the long walk there, down the Coffee, up the Promenade near the Anglican church across from the courthouse. There, we will be schooled in many things, but most significantly in the racial work of literature, whose most abiding feature will be our absence, on the one hand, and our eternal subjugate presence, on the other hand.

To learn the literature of the conqueror is both obligatory and bureaucratic; any aesthetic value is absent, except as a directive. This is what literature is. This is what beauty is. These are the people deserving of a beautiful life. These are the travails that accompany their achievement of that life. This is not you. This literature—that is, the literature of the conqueror—has no value, if we are to think of value as enriching, nor is it beautiful. Its position as beautiful or valuable is iterative. But one does not know that until later. One only suspects it, through the fight-or-flight response one experiences as this literature is administered and ingested with admonition and shame. C.L.R. James's *Minty*

Alley (1936) and George Lamming's *In the Castle of My Skin* (1953) are not yet—and will not be for some time—part of formal instruction. You do not appear in colonial literature as its subject but as its implied or obvious degraded other, and so this work arrives with loss or absence. You are in it as sacrifice, as detritus. You must make a massively dishonest claim as its subject. It is a claim that exposes you constantly to the insupportableness of the claim. This literature arrives with its forbidding, with its closed portal; and because it is a portal, there is a glass through which you are instructed to look. And you are aware that you are looking, since it arrives with a signal; it arrives posing as a gift and a remedy. You are thought to be incomplete without this literature, and though you are unaware that you are incomplete, you will become aware as soon as you look. You in your life, you know that this literature, these instructions, will arrive, since the ground is laid for their arrival in the material conditions of your life, even if that life is very young. Physical portals like streets, buildings and the general discourse around you have already laid out the architecture of your living, of your existence. These streets, buildings, are predestined. We had to learn these instructions in the order and form they were given. Many of us were referred to as "bright" if we succeeded in regurgitating this teaching in the right order and correct form as it was given. Everyone strove to be "bright."

Colonialism is such a pessimistic discourse, especially for the colonized—it is full of hopelessness about one's future, about one's daily appearances. One not only has to confront daily living—the acts of walking, thinking, being on the surface of the planet—one must also confront an imposition of form, of

187

symmetry with the ruling relations. The small restrictive world of the colonial overlays the big world, narrowing philosophical possibilities held in place by power structures undergirded by narrative. But to paraphrase both Audre Lorde (on using the tools of the "master") and Friedrich Engels (on political economy) one cannot be content to take the terms of the literary as they are, and to operate with them, failing to see that by doing so we are therefore confined "within the narrow circle of ideas expressed by those terms."[132]

My novel *At the Full and Change of the Moon* is an historical novel. But to call it an historical novel is also not quite correct because it refuses the linearity that accompanies ideas of history. The genealogical table drawn at the opening of the novel contains the molecular *and* the historical—it maps a transformation of the individual and collective lives of one family, in and as diaspora. (This novel was my attempt at extrapolating from Gramsci's molecular to the historical.)

In that family photograph being sent to England, we are not all what might be called blood sisters—we are three sisters and a cousin—but we are four sisters, nevertheless. We are sisters who live with their grandmother and grandfather and uncles, and occasionally an aunt or two, and a second cousin and several other first cousins. And our sociality is constructed through what is called "pumpkin-vine family"—a genealogy of survival.

So, too, the genealogy of *At the Full and Change of the Moon* is one of survival, improvisation and circumlocution—of pumpkin-vine family. As the narrative references this cosmos, it begins with a woman whose major act in the book is an act of freeing herself and others from slavery by mass suicide. Her small vanity, which is how the narrator describes it, is to bear a child (Bola) who might exist in the world free. We trace the thread of her progeny—and her decision to die and to send her child into a world that she herself will not meet—on the vicarious, idiosyncratic map of genealogy. The major philosophical point in the book is that the descendants of the people who were enslaved owe nothing; they owe no account of their life and world to the people who enslaved their grandmother and grandfather, nor do they owe the contemporary world for/or about their existence. They do not even owe it attention. The genealogy is a self-description: they are free of being property, and free of property as pinion that holds them in the world. The familial descriptions are errant, attributive of desires, intentions and actions. They refuse linearity of the sort that might reference wealth or social status—after all, they are the machinery on which wealth and social status are built. *Full and Change*'s genealogy is therefore one of personal ephemera—a table that is understandable and adherent to the time of the Middle Passage.

Marie Ursule, died 1824.

Kamena, marooned to his last direction, 1824.

Bola born 1821, died 1921, who was Maria Ursule's vanity and whose eyes wept an ocean and who loved whales.

The one unrecalled, born 1841. The ones left in the sea, born 1846, 1849, 1850. The one she made in the dry season, born 1856.

Eugenia, the one who went to Bonaire in a basket, born 1858. Rafael Simon, the one who loved gold things and who was taken to the main (Venezuela), born 1860.

Emmanuel Greaves, born 1905, married Cordelia Rojas, born 1903. Children—Hannah, Gabriel, Alicia.

The one who was taken in a hurricane, born 1869, taken 1875. The one who loved dolls, born 1863. The one she washed out with lime, born 1865. The one who ran to the Rupununi, born 1875. The one who pointed to the sea saying, "Boto Bayena" and who loved to iron clothes and who was taken to Curaçao, born 1865.

Dovett, born 1890, died 1925. Dovett, born 1920, died 1978.

Maya, born 1952. Adrian, born 1959.

The girl who was flooded in everything, born 1987.

The one who stole her footsteps, born 1869, who left and found Terre Bouillante without looking, 1881. Augusta, the one for the blind man whose head she loved, born 1881.

Private Sones, born 1898.

Dear Mama, born 1919.

The sisters who went to England born 1936 and 1937. Sese, born 1939. Priest, born 1940. Job, born 1945. Eula, born 1957.

Bola, born 1982.

The table's narration unpins Marie Ursule's progeny from any of the references to a colonial/capitalist world. It contains no references to the world that enslaved their grandmother or great grandmother. And when these protagonists encounter those structures, they are, of course, often destroyed—or they make their way somehow. The novel is, too, about the characters' continued encounters and reckonings with that world, a world that put a ten-pound weight around their great-great-grandmother's leg for rebellion.

While they cannot but live in the world that they live in, Marie Ursule's succeeding generations inherit her *sense of freedom*, which is rebellion in every way possible against the structures that would imprison them. It makes for a life of epiphanies. As well as a life of losses.

These characters are, many of them, under duress, and they therefore sometimes find themselves utterly vulnerable to attack and self-immolation. The gift that Marie Ursule gives them is this: the gift of feeling themselves sovereign. And whether the structures they live under pathologize or sociologize them really doesn't matter to them. They inhabit their sovereignty. What she has given them is her act: that act of refusal of the forms of life ascribed to the enslaved; her act that rejects all forms of that transaction. This is the refusal she has gifted them. They do not always inhabit it, but it is their possibility.

My first autobiography of the childhood photograph told of the diasporas gathered around, and inside, the photographer's studio. Mr. Wong is from the Chinese diaspora. His forebears may have been brought to Trinidad as indentured labour from Guangdong Province, beginning in 1806. His art rips itself away from that utility, takes this photograph.

Another diaspora of people transported as indentured labour is referenced in the Indian cinema outside, nearby, along a street close to the library. Indian indentured labour interpolates the photograph of the four little girls. And in my novel, Rabindranath Ragoonanan interpolates Marie Ursule's genealogy as "the blind man whose head she loved." Outside of Mr. Wong's studio and along the High Street, along Mucurapo Street, along Lord Street, there are people who trace their presence to this post-slavery slavery. The British called it indentureship. I find Private Sones (in my novel, Ragoonanan's son, Marie Ursule's great-grandson) in the record of the First World War—he will go to England and then to Palestine to fight the Turks on Damieh Hill. His efforts at assimilation into the "mother country" are a failure, however, and he returns to pay penance to his waiting and heterogenous self.

The genealogy's narrative does not ask for synchronicity or reconciliation with the structures of domination lived and encountered. I was not interested in narrating a struggle to overcome, nor one of perseverance in the face of crisis and catastrophe. I was interested in a narrative of conscious, wilful living. Sones walks the town of Culebra in his suffocating English suit as his own penance for being duped historically and for living in empire's elaborations and nostalgias.

The artist Fred Wilson, in an essay on museums, writes, "The aesthetic anesthetizes the historic and keeps this imperial view within the museum and continues the dislocation of what these objects are about."[133] We may read the literature of empire in the same way. Nostalgia is what keeps empire's literature fundamental to discourse and discursive practices. And critiques launched against the museums that hold objects of empire as well as critiques of the literature of empire are required to first acknowledge an ascribed value to these things—not merely value as the literature of empire, but some objective value outside of the work's production as imperial object.

Arguments against returning stolen artistic or reliquary items, for instance, are arguments for the right to imperial nostalgia. One might ask: How can the stolen bodies be returned? And the stolen life? The insistence on keeping the symbols of conquest, as if these are distinct from conquest, as if some other extrinsic value were attached to them—that is a longing for empire; that is insisting on the logic of the empire in the quotidian. These artifacts are evidence of conquest, they are symbols of the pleasures of conquest, and their location, and the regard given to them in those locations, repeats the acts of violence and gives a sense of invigoration to imperial practices. Racial tropes pervade the argument that these items will not be taken care of, if returned; but in truth, arguments around these items still strive to hold on to the symbols of our death or the method of our death. They are a refusal to allow another meaning to inhabit the artifacts—both the original meanings and future meanings. These arguments are an insistence that such artifacts remain in imperialist, rather than liberatory, cosmologies.

If we say that these imperialist texts have an untouchable status as objects of aesthetic value and if we say that literature cultivates the human, inspires and activates ethical living; if those verities are to be held; if we are to take these generalities that describe what literature does as "common"—then the experience of a Black reader like me cannot be anything but the cultivation of a continuous dread. And it must be acknowledged that books such as those texts where scenes of Black life are a stage for white ambition and desire and progress have a profound, stultifying, disorienting effect upon a reader like me. Such accounts in these novels of imperialism only elicit anxiety from readers like me, since as we read, *we* encounter *time* in the novel even as we simultaneously are meant to encounter these verities and generalities. A white reader encounters the flow of time, we encounter stasis. We know the duration of slavery, and we know no other life is possible for the Black protagonist/subject, no trajectory to freedom, since the novel's bedrock of landscape, character and desire self-evidently contain us as chattel. The range of emotion in these works is limiting, in that there can only be grief and fear and melancholy, not happiness or love or wonder (except the wonder in horror). In other words, the full range of emotions and repair that a novel might offer and is said to offer are, *a priori*, foreclosed to a reader like me. And put another way, in these scenes, Black dread is ligatured to white experience— one could even say this is done typographically, since the effect on a reader like me is to notice the formation of the ligatures in each sentence and experience them as a cataclysm. If we say that a Black reader like me ought not to notice that cataclysm, ought not to notice that the text is active, but only acknowledge its assignment through the lens of refined taste, then a reader like me is, to quote Gikandi in his *Slavery and the Culture of Taste*, "excluded from the domain of modern reason, aesthetic judgement and the culture of taste."[134]

The work of narrativizing the life of Black people is difficult, as that life sits at a cardinal coordinate of capital and white power; it is located in the racist schema that capital and white power describe. The task of the writer, of a writer like me, whether of fiction or non-fiction, or of casual or bureaucratic texts, is to narrate our own consciousnesses, to retrieve a life in the register of the social and the political, and not in the register of pathologies or the pathological.

Roy DeCarava's collection of photographs and words, *the sound i saw*, calls us to the synesthetic space of our living. The collection gathers a sense of where and how to look at, and to feel with, Black people. The work moves through the sensorium of blackness, from bare streets to creative virtuosic interiors. DeCarava's musicians and ordinary people, men, women, boys, girls, are photographed with their intellectual and theoretical gifts, in contemplation, in study, in calculation, in perhaps worry or wonderment, or intent—*in medias res*—mid-song, mid-composition, mid-collaboration, mid-drawing a hopscotch box, mid-practice, mid-stillness. The black and white photographs are so deeply complicated in light and shadow that they do not belong to the viewer-reader-interpreter, but to the subject. Any possible racist interpretations are trifling against the genius of Black living at the centre of the works. The cavernous streets and the burnt, broken tenements against the lone boys; the massive odds, and then the close contemplative face of Coltrane, the even closer faces of Marian Anderson and Billie Holiday mid-song; then there is the dressed-up small child standing on the clear pavement, the desultory tenement looming. The physical labours and creative labours alternate, as do the interior and the exterior. In his photographs, DeCarava refuses the interruption in every minute, every exposure. His photographs place the interruption in its true proportion to the lived whole.

The interdisciplinary painter Torkwase Dyson has a series of works called *Hypershapes* where she draws, imagines, the myriad and intricate angles, aspects, distances and scales of "looking" from the holds of the ships of the Middle Passage. She draws/imagines hundreds of designs of the gaze that analyzed and exceeded the hold. One imagines alongside her the millions of calculations on those thousands of voyages, the millions of sightlines, the trillions of imagined geometries of the people in the hold. What would it be to house a literature in these geometries, I wonder.

And Gwendolyn Brooks answers. Her *Maud Martha* is one such example in fiction of a narrative attending to its own expression, attending to describing its consciousness. Here in *Maud Martha* is a consciousness unimpeded by the demand to locate itself adjacent to a spectator who wishes to dislocate that consciousness or make it inanimate and tangential. The mindbox opens in the reader. Brooks arranges an ordinary life, without a spectator who is invested in violence as the only mode of, or code for, referencing that life: "Up the street, mixed in the wind, blew the children, and turned the corner onto the brownish-red brick school court. It was wonderful. Bits of pink, of blue, white, yellow, green, purple, brown, black, carried by jerky little stems of brown or yellow or brown-black, blew by the unhandsome gray and decay of the double-apartment buildings, past the little plots of dirt and scanty grass. . . . There were lives in the buildings. Past the tiny lives the children blew."[135]

The children in Brooks's description may be very similar to the four children in the photograph at Mr. Wong's studio. Their disarray is as yet unattended by the violence of colonial pedagogy. Violence surely hovers over and presages their presence, but their desires and the alertness of their beings are the foregrounded, crucial details. Brooks's narrator *sees* these children. There is a sense in which the children in Mr. Wong's photograph, too, escape the reference of colony—they have yet to be collected. Their escape is recorded in their discombobulation, their fear, their panic, their crying, their distance—signs of their sovereignty—their resistance to being gathered.

The beauty of *Maud Martha* is that it assumes this sovereign point of view, and it is in this *address* that it locates its protagonist and the world. The character Maud Martha's ruminations, too, occupy the central philosophical ground, not the partial or adjunct. Brooks writes:

People have to choose something decently constant to depend on, thought Maud Martha. People must have something to lean on. But the love of a single person was not enough. Not only was personal love itself, however good, a thing that varied from week to week, from second to second, but the parties to it were likely, for example, to die, any minute, or otherwise be parted, or destroyed. . . . Could be nature, which had a seed, or root, or an element (what do you want to call it) of constancy, under all that system of change. Of course, to say "system" at all implied arrangement, and therefore some order of constancy.[136]

Brooks suggests another "we" entirely, one that beckons a reader such as me with familiarity, with a proposition, with an invitation to construct the narrative's coherence without requiring the presumption of abject location. It is a "we" into which this reader might be gathered.

In his short story "Rivers," in *Counternarratives,* John Keene offers a counter to Mark Twain's *Huckleberry Finn.* At the centre of Keene's story is James Rivers, whom we meet after the Civil War. James Rivers is not the Jim of Twain's book. Rivers recounts the time when a reporter who is supposed to interview him about "the war and his service in it" instead asks him a question about "that boy" (Huck Finn), whom he has seen only twice in the intervening forty years. The story begins: "What I'd like to hear about, the reporter starts in, is the time you and that little boy . . . and I silence him again with a turn of my head thinking to myself. . . ."[137] And what follows is a partial list of the places where he was and battles he fought, in what he names "the first great war for *our* freedom."[138] This *our*, italicized in Keene's text, is very clear—the *our* references Black freedom, and it stands counter to that violent *we* that I wrote of earlier.

The reporter's question and its narrative demand want to return Rivers to a time and place he has worked to forget—or, perhaps more to the point, to return him to a point that is not the point of his life. The reporter's question would take him back to Twain's narrative, in which the white boy/man and not James Rivers is at the centre, but Rivers has his own narrative. And Keene gives us James Rivers's narrative, at first by way of a face turned away in refusal, and then by way of a remembered encounter with Tom (Sawyer) in which the necessary dissimulation, evidenced in the grammar of the past conditional, is on the page, in successive paragraphs that begin: "I thought to tell the boy," "I thought to say," "I thought to say," "I thought to recount," "I thought to narrate," "I think to conclude."[139] The body of the story tells of Rivers' life, not of his performance in a picaresque *about* a white boy. Like Brooks, Keene makes explicit the act of blowing life into the collapsed world of coloniality.

This ending is about a house

Here is a house with a window, like the kind of window of fresh expectations in the first paragraph of Merle Hodge's novel *Crick Crack, Monkey*: "We had posted ourselves at the front window, standing on a chair. Tantie said we were stupid, for they might not come back till next morning or maybe even for days but if we wanted to stand on tiptoe at the window for a week that was all right by her as long as we got down once in a while to bathe."[140]

Sometimes this house is far back in a treed place, sometimes it is near a river, or near an ocean, or up an uneven path. Sometimes it is among many houses like it. Sometimes this is not a house but a factory, a long barrack where, long ago, cacao or copra was put to dry on a massive tray, and during the day the roof was rolled away for the sun to do its work. There's an image of this in the 2021 exhibition *Fragments of Epic Memory* at the Art Gallery of Ontario. In the exhibit and catalogue there is a photograph of a small girl with a wicker basket sitting atop a roof. It is the kind of roof that serves as a drying tray for cacao or copra. In the day, when the sun is shining, the roof cover is pulleyed open to reveal the drying trays. There's a boy raking the cacao in one of the trays, and three men standing in other trays.

There is the scent of fermenting and drying cacao for miles, I'm sure. People live below in barracks. And the same things happened there as happened in my house—mornings, evenings, afternoons. But that photograph was taken a long time ago. This house, like mine, has its origins in what George Lamming called "the site of production" that was the Americas, the Caribbean archipelago. Copra barracks or single dwellings, these architectures arose out of no great intention to house people one cared for or loved. These architectures come out of slavery. These architectures were/are convenient to capital. A desire to live in a house, a relief at a certain landscape, a doorway, a door, steps and floorboards, may index a dangerous or uncanny nostalgia. But other things were and are made in these houses. Things like life. Conviviality. Affective things—hair was combed, bodies were bathed, meals were prepared, names were given, music was made and sung. And people were loved and mourned. Plots were laid against the plantation. Plots were made against the state. Plans were made for living after. All of this, and more, happened in a house with a window, and a curtain moving in the wind.

This house is a single dwelling. This house is the house I want to live in. This house is the house I have always wanted to live in. This is not the house that I lived in. It is the house that I saw and was in love with. It is a house that I am familiar with, a country house, a wooden house. There are two windows on each side, a peaked roof that slopes and flattens to the back. There is a galvanized roof that amplifies the sound of rain. There is a verandah to the front leading from three doors, two that are louvred to the top, and the central door bifurcated so that the top half opens, and you can lean on the bottom half, talking to someone outside. On this house, the galvanized steel is rusting, caking off in oxblood porous pieces. The verandah is worn, with wood lice runnels on its surface, but it is still solid in parts. The kitchen is at the back of the house. The enamel dishes and pots are laid out on a sideboard with a cloth over them. The kitchen has a window that is hinged on the top, and you push it open with a broomstick. There is what's called a safe in the drawing room, with all the ware cups for when there's company. The house is on stilts, and sometimes you can go underneath, you can keep dogs there or chickens, or goats or nothing. Sometimes the house is not on stilts. From inside the house, through some of the floorboards, you can sometimes see the ground below, you can sometimes feel the motion of the air, a breeze or so. Or see a slithering snake or lizard. If you put your ear to the floorboards, you can hear the wind. The floors of the rooms are well polished, there are Morris chairs, and a wooden table and two raffia seated chairs. On the table there is a lamp. In the bedroom there is a bed and a stand with a large wash jug and a basin near the window. At first this jug and basin, yellow and white with flowers, are ceramic and precious. Then, broken, the wash jug elicits grief, as it was the only fine thing in the house. The new wash jug is enamel, red-rimmed at the lip; the wash basin is blue-lipped. This is my house. And there are other houses like this not far away, set beyond a road. Or near a road. And any road is gravel and far from something. There are trees and vines around these houses, or flowers. Sometimes this house is up a steep hill. Any houses that come after cannot match this house for safety or difficulty.

There are no conversations more private than the conversations in this house and houses like these. There are no worries more grieving, no comfort more assuaging. This house is a retreat and a rescue.

This house of mine is small, brief, it is likely to fall down. But if it does, it falls on one side or another, never quite falling enough to be uninhabitable for us. The steps to the door rot, or they are beaten away by rain. The roof leaks and is covered temporarily by wood or galvanized steel. A patch of some kind. Or a bucket is placed under the leak, only to have another leak open if the occupant thinks that's all there is to do. So, a bowl is added to catch the new water. And a remark that rainwater is good. This house most often leans. In any direction. But there is a curtain at the doorway. And there are curtains at the windows. When there is a breeze, the curtain blows in and out, gently.

This is the house I've always lived in. It is the house I've duplicated in every house I've lived in, every apartment, every room. I can't really live in this house, but to be precise some parts of me always live in this house, and some parts of me long to live in this house, obviously. I look at this house with the feeling that I am deserting someone, someone who needs me.

I have gone off out of the house, out of the photograph, gone off to read and ruin my eyes. And when I look back, I see this house and all it has salvaged from the site of production.

Now I wonder if the ending of *Minty Alley* has always informed the way I look into houses when I pass by them at night. Haynes stands outside the house in Minty Alley, where he used to live; another family now occupies the house, a child is playing a piano in the drawing room. "The front and windows were open and from the street he could see into the drawing-room. . . . Over and over, she played it, while he stood outside, looking in at the window and thinking of old times."[141]

Perhaps the whole of *Minty Alley* resonated through my own Mon Repos Scheme, the backyards, the hopscotched streets. And me, like Haynes, observing, but taking only a small part in the cut and thrust, in the passions of life. Except, as narrative.

Acknowledgements

Gratitude is not enough, yet it is all I have: Christina Sharpe, Rinaldo Walcott, Canisia Lubrin, for all the conversations, ongoing and limitless; Tina Campt, who gave me time at Princeton; Saidiya Hartman, who talked me through in Venice and beyond; Torkwase Dyson, who showed me scale from Toronto to the desert; Lynn Henry, Eric Chinski, editors who gave me rigorous, copious, generous and valuable notes, and time; Sarah Chalfant, Charles Buchan, Jackie Ko, Kristi Murray at The Wylie Agency, who take my side and make a way, always; Jan Anderson, meticulous reader and citation guru; Emma Lockhart and Hilary Lo, detailers of the manuscript; *Brick Magazine*, where the part of this book about Werner Herzog's *Aguirre, the Wrath of God* first appeared; Centre for Literatures, University of Alberta, and the 2019 Kreisel Lecture, where part of "an autobiography" was first delivered and published; All Souls College Oxford, where the part of this book about "violent elisions" was delivered as The Atlantic Slavery and its Aftermath Lecture 2024.

Permissions and Credits

Page 10. "What We Can Learn from Elizabeth Barrett Browning's Years in Lockdown," by Fiona Sampson, from *The Guardian*. Copyright Guardian News & Media Ltd 2024. Used under license.

Pages 25–27. Excerpts from *Beyond a Boundary* by C.L.R. James published by Vintage Classics. Copyright © Executor to the Estate of C L R James, 1963. Reprinted by permission of The Random House Group Limited.

Page 97. "Truss to push ahead with low-tax economy despite calls for caution," by Peter Walker and Rupert Neate, from *The Guardian*. Copyright Guardian News & Media Ltd 2024. Used under license.

Pages 118–125. Excerpts from *Foe* by J.M. Coetzee. Copyright © J. M. Coetzee, 1986. Reprinted by permission of The Random House Group Limited. Ebook and audio reproduction used by permission of Peter Lampack Agency, Inc.

Pages 130–136, 139. Excerpts from *Crusoe's Footprint* by Patrick Chamoiseau, translated by Jeffrey Landon Allen and Charly Verstraet, pp. 13, 14, 17, 20, 22, 24, 29, 30, 45, 109, 110. © 2022 by the Rector and Visitors of the University of Virginia. © Editions Gallimard, Paris, 2012 *L'Empreinte A Crusoe*. Reprinted by permission of the University of Virginia Press and Editions Gallimard.

Pages 140–141. Excerpt from *Palace of the Peacock* by Wilson Harris, published by Faber and Faber Ltd. Used with permission.

Pages 165–166, 206–207. Excerpts from *Minty Alley* by C.L.R. James published by Penguin. Copyright © C. L. R. James, 1936, 1971. Reprinted by permission of Penguin Books Limited.

Notes

1. Ficre Ghebreysus, *Solitary Boat in Red and Blue*, Ficre Ghebreyesus Fine Art, LLC. Ficre-ghebreyesus.com/painting
2. Dionne Brand, *Inventory* (Toronto: McClelland and Stewart, 2006), 92.
3. Remedios Varo, *Exploration of the Sources of the Orinoco River*, 1959
4. Ever Given, one of the largest container ships in the world. Operated by Ever Green marine (Taiwan), registered in Panama, technically managed by Bernhard Schulte Ship Management, a German Company.
5. Jon Gambrell, "Massive cargo ship turns sideways, blocks Egypt's Suez Canal." Associated Press (23 March 2021).
6. Bibby Stockholm was an engineless barge used as an accommodation vessel. In April 2023 the governments of the United Kingdom used it to house asylum seekers at Portland Port in Dorset.
7. Convict Hulks or Prison Hulks were prison ships, the first was called the "Justitia."
8. Mike Thomson, "Migrant Crisis: Tunisian Fisherman Finds Dead Bodies in His Net," BBC, June 20, 2023.
9. J.M.W. Turner's 1840 painting was known as *The Slave Ship*.
10. Ruskin, John. "Of Water as painted by Turner." *Modern Painters Vol. I* (1846): 537–73.
11. Saskia Sassen, *Expulsions: Brutality and Complexity in the Global Economy* (Cambridge: The Belknap Press of Harvard University Press, 2014).
12. Fiona Sampson, "What We Can Learn from Elizabeth Barrett Browning's Years in Lockdown," *Guardian*, February 15, 2021.
13. Harriet Jacobs, *Incidents in the Life of a Slave Girl: Written by Herself* (Boston: Thayer and Eldridge, 1861).
14. Simone Leigh, Loophole of retreat: Venice Biennale, U.S. Pavilion, October 7–9, 2022. https://www.labiennale.org/en/art/2022/united-states-america.

15. Toni Morrison, *Beloved* (New York: Penguin Books, 1988). Tsitsi Dangarembga, *Nervous Conditions* (London, The Women's Press, 1988). Sam Selvon, *The Lonely Londoners* (Toronto: TSAR Publications, 1991). Edwidge Danticat, *The Farming of Bones* (New York: Soho Press, 1998). John Keene, *Counternarratives* (New York: New Directions Publishing Corp, 2015).

16. Cunard was a popular passenger shipping line established in 1839 by Samuel Cunard with the slogan, "Getting there is half the fun."

17. Samuel Selvon, *The Lonely Londoners* (Toronto: TSAR Publications, 1991), 7.

18. C.L.R. James, *Beyond a Boundary* (Durham: Duke University Press, 1993), 39.

19. Ibid., 39.

20. Ibid., 39–40.

21. Ibid., 40.

22. Ibid., 40–41.

23. Ibid., 41–42.

24. Lisa Lowe, *The Intimacies of Four Continents* (Durham, NC: Duke University Press, 2015), 81.

25. William Makepeace Thackeray, *Vanity Fair* (London: J.M. Dent & Sons, 1930), 13.

26. Ibid., 8.

27. Ibid., 5.

28. Edward Said, *Culture and Imperialism* (London: Vintage, 1994), 73.

29. *Treaty of Amiens*, 1802. Signed during the Napoleonic Wars after which war abated for a little over a year. The stakes of these wars were colonial possession. At Amiens the French took back all their colonies. The British took Sri Lanka (then Ceylon) and Trinidad from the Dutch and the Spanish respectively. The Cape of Good Hope went to Holland.

30. William Makepeace Thackeray, *The History of Henry Esmond, Esq.* (New York: MacMillan, 1902), vii.

31. Simon Gikandi, "Aesthetic Reflection and the Colonial Event: The Work of Art in the Age of Slavery," *Journal of the International Institute* 4, no. 3 (Spring/Summer 1997): https://quod.lib.umich.edu/j/jii/4750978.0004 .306?view=text;rgn=main. [Accessed 2.14.2024]

32. Thackeray, *Henry Esmond, Esq.*, ix.

33. Ibid., x, viii.

34. Sylvia Wynter, "Novel and History, Plot and Plantation," *Savacou* 5 (June 1971), 95.

35. Édouard Glissant, *Poetics of Relation* (Ann Arbor: University of Michigan Press, 1997), 117.

36. Dionne Brand, "At the Lisbon Plate," in *Sans Souci, and Other Stories* (Stratford: Williams-Wallace, 1988), 112.

37. Christina Sharpe, personal communication, October 2018.

38. Charlotte Brontë, *Jane Eyre* (Oxford: New Windmill Classics, 1993), 188.

39. Ibid., 198–199.

40. Ibid., 219.

41. Ibid., 225.

42. Jean Rhys, *Wide Sargasso Sea* (London: World Books, 1967), 160.

43. Rinaldo Walcott, *The Long Emancipation* (Durham: Duke University Press, 2021), 55.

44. Brontë, *Jane Eyre*, 61.

45. Kevin Adonis Browne, "Preface to a Memory of Dominica," *Brick* 103 (Summer 2019): 91–92.

46. Sven Lindqvist, *A History of Bombing* (New York: The New Press, 2001), 31.

47. Virginia Woolf, *A Room of One's Own* (London: Hogarth Press, 1935), 98.

48. Aphra Behn, *Oroonoko, or The Royal Slave* (New York: W.W. Norton and Company, 1973), 1–4.

49. Ibid., 3–4.

50. Ibid., 6.

51. Ibid., 8.

52. Ibid., 7.

53. Ibid., 38.

54. Ibid., 40–41.

55. Ibid., 42.

56. Ibid., 42–43.

57. Ibid., 43.

58. Ibid., 54, 57.

59. Ibid., 57.

60. Ibid., 60–61.

61. Ibid., 68.

62. Ibid., 77.

63. Zakiyyah Iman Jackson, *Becoming Human* (New York: New York University Press, 2020), 35.

64. Buzz Bissinger, "Tiger in the Rough," *Vanity Fair*, February 2010.

65. Moore, Wendy L., and Joyce M. Bell. "Embodying the White Racial

Frame: The (in)Significance of Barack Obama." *The Journal of Race & Policy*, vol. 6, no. 1, 2010, pp. 122–137.

66. Daniel Defoe, *The Life and Adventures of Robinson Crusoe* (Boston: D. Lothrop and Company, 1884), 4.
67. Ibid., 14.
68. Ibid., 15.
69. Ibid., 26.
70. Ibid., 26.
71. Dionne Brand, *A Map to the Door of No Return* (Toronto: Vintage Canada, 2001), 207. There are many instances of this recorded in the diaries of Père Labat. "They are going to the colonies to convert savages."
72. Defoe, *Robinson Crusoe*, 30.
73. Ibid., 31.
74. Ibid., 35–36.
75. Peter Walker and Rupert Neate, "Truss to Push Ahead with Low-Tax Economy Despite Calls for Caution," *Guardian*, September 4, 2022.
76. Defoe, *Robinson Crusoe*, 89–90.
77. Ibid., 90.
78. W.E.B. DuBois, "The Souls of White Folk," *Darkwater: Voices from Within the Veil* (New York: Harcourt, Brace and Company, 1921), 30.
79. Defoe, *Robinson Crusoe*, 155.
80. Ibid., 159.
81. Ibid., 192–193.
82. Ibid., 160–161.
83. Ibid., 190.
84. Matthew Watson, "Crusoe, Friday and the Raced Market Frame of Orthodox Economics Textbooks," *New Political Economy* 23, no. 5 (September 2018): 544–59.
85. Defoe, *Robinson Crusoe*, 267–268.
86. J.M. Coetzee, *Foe* (New York: Penguin Books, 1987), 18.
87. Ibid., 23.
88. Ibid., 30.
89. Ibid., 37.
90. Ibid., 39.
91. Ibid., 68.
92. Ibid., 45.
93. Ibid., 142.
94. Ibid., 143.

95. Ibid., 149.
96. James Weldon Johnson, *The Autobiography of an Ex-colored Man* (New York: Hill and Wang, 1960), 21.
97. Ibid., 21–22.
98. Herman Melville, *Benito Cereno* (New York: Dover Publications, 1990), 103–104.
99. Ibid., 102–103.
100. Achebe, Chinua. "African Author Chinua Achebe." Interview by Bill Moyers. September 29, 1988. www.billmoyers.com/content/chinua-achebe.
101. Patrick Chamoiseau, *Crusoe's Footprint*, trans. Jeffrey Landon Allen and Charly Verstraet (Charlottesville, VA: University of Virginia Press, 2022), 13–14.
102. Ibid., 17.
103. Ibid., 20.
104. Ibid., 22, 24.
105. Ibid., 29–30.
106. Ibid., 45.
107. Ibid., 109–110.
108. Anna Julia Cooper, *A Voice From the South* (New York: Oxford University Press, 1988), 103.
109. Toni Morrison, *Beloved* (New York: Penguin Books, 1988), 5.
110. Toni Morrison, "Home," *The House that Race Built* (New York: Pantheon Books, 1997), 10.
111. Chamoiseau, *Crusoe's Footprint*, 162.
112. Wilson Harris, *Palace of the Peacock* (London: Faber & Faber, 1960), 51–52.
113. Kenneth Ramchand, afterword to Harris, *Palace of the Peacock*, 130.
114. Édouard Glissant, *Caribbean Discourse* (Charlottesville: University Press of Virginia, 1989), 145.
115. Sancho, Ignatius. *Letters of the Late Ignatius Sancho, an African: To which are Prefixed, Memoirs of his Life* (London: J. Nichols and C. Dilly, 1783), 96–98.
116. Quobna Ottobah Cuguano, *Thoughts and Sentiments on the Evil of Slavery* (London: Penguin Classics, 1999), 10–12.
117. Jane Austen, *Mansfield Park Volume II* (London: J. Murray, 1816), 5.
118. Ibid., 62. Ibid., *Volume II*, 9, 13.
119. Edward Said, *Culture and Imperialism* (London: Vintage, 1994), 112.
120. Gikandi, Simon. *Slavery and the Culture of Taste* (Princeton: Princeton University Press, 2011), 149.
121. Lamming, George. "The Present Future of Caribbean Literature and

Cultural Studies Symposium" Part 2. An Academic Symposium in honor of Sandra Pouchet Paquet, Professor Emerita of English at the University of Miami, March 2010, https://www.youtube.com/watch?v=7zc5L2ugw&t=15s (5:30-6:30).

122. Said, *Culture and Imperialism*, 106, 115.

123. Dionne Brand, *Inventory* (Toronto: McClelland & Stewart, 2006), 3.

124. Ibid., 3.

125. Kim Johnson, *The Illustrated Story of Pan* (Port of Spain: University of Trinidad and Tobago Press, 2011), 23.

126. C.L.R. James, *Minty Alley* (London: New Beacon Books Ltd., 1971), 22.

127. Ibid., 206.

128. Ibid., 226.

129. Richard Wright, introduction to *In the Castle of My Skin*, by George Lamming (New York: Collier Books, 1953), vii, vii.

130. DeCarava, Roy and Langston Hughes, *The Sweet Flypaper of Life* (New York: Hill and Wang, 1967), 92.

131. Professor Emeritus Dr. William Belhouewer, personal communication, Fall 2019.

132. Friedrich Engels, Preface to English edition *Capital* by Karl Marx (Moscow: Progress Publishers, 1887), 20. "Political Economy has generally been content to take, just as they were, the terms of commercial and industrial life, and to operate with them, entirely failing to see that by so doing, it confined itself within the narrow circle of ideas expressed by those terms."

133. Karp, Ivan and Fred Wilson. "Constructing the Spectacle of Culture in Museums" in *Thinking About Exhibitions*, edited by Ressa Greenberg, Bruce W Ferguson, Sandy Nairne. (New York: Routledge, 1996), 181.

134. Simon Gikandi, *Slavery and the Culture of Taste* (Princeton, Princeton University Press, 2011), 5.

135. Gwendolyn Brooks, *Maud Martha* (New York: Harper and Brothers Publishers, 1953), 5.

136. Ibid., 100–101.

137. John Keene, "Rivers," in *Counternarratives* (New York: New Directions Publishing, 2015), 219.

138. Ibid., 219.

139. Ibid., 222, 223, 224, 225.

140. Merle Hodge, *Crick Crack, Monkey* (Kingston: Heinemann Publishers Caribbean Ltd., 1981), 1.

141. C.L.R. James, *Minty Alley* (London: New Beacon Books Ltd., 1971), 244.

A Note About the Author

Dionne Brand is the award-winning author of twenty-three books of poetry, fiction, and nonfiction. Her twelve books of poetry include *Land to Light On*; *thirsty*; *Inventory*; *Ossuaries*; *The Blue Clerk: Ars Poetica in 59 Versos*; and *Nomenclature: New and Collected Poems*. Her six works of fiction include *At the Full and Change of the Moon*; *What We All Long For*; *Love Enough*; and *Theory*. Her nonfiction work includes *Bread Out of Stone* and *A Map to the Door of No Return: Notes to Belonging*.

Brand is the recipient of numerous literary prizes, among them the Griffin Poetry Prize, the Toronto Book Award, the Trillium Book Award, and the 2021 Windham-Campbell Prize for Fiction. She is a University Professor Emerita at the University of Guelph. She lives in Toronto, Canada.